What Must the

Church of

Christ

Do To Be Saved?

Leroy Garrett

What Must the Church of Christ Do to be Saved?

Leroy Garrett

Copyright © 2011

Table of Contents

Publisher's Note

With the collaboration of the author, we have assembled in a single work twenty essays written from January of 1991 to October of 1992 and published in *Restoration Review*. Although the essays appeared as a numerical series under the title, "What must the Church of Christ do to be saved?," each essay contained a suggested topic which usually appeared in italic typeface. These have been used as chapter titles in this book.

We have included in appendices (I) "An Address to Churches of Christ," by Barton W. Stone, (II) A letter from the Quaker Avenue Church of Christ, (III) a letter from the Broadway Church of Christ, and (IV) a personal email regarding unity efforts in Lubbock, Texas, in which several hundred representatives of all three branches of the Stone-Campbell Movement convened and signed a unity pledge, a copy of which is included. The appendices are linked to specific references in the essays and are included with the approval of the author. We have also added footnotes which give the current location on the Internet of documents to which the author makes reference.

Dr. Leroy Garrett is a graduate of Abilene Christian University, Princeton Theological Seminary, and Harvard University where he earned the Ph.D. He is a retired professor of philosophy, history, and religion and has taught at several colleges, including Bethany College, Texas Woman's University, and Dallas Christian College. For thirty-four years he edited the monthly journal, *Restoration Review*, following six years as editor of *Bible Talk*. He is the author of *The Stone-Campbell Movement*, the story of the American Restoration Movement, published by College Press, and an autobiographical work, *A Lover's Quarrel*, published by A.C.U. Press. He has lectured at colleges and churches of all three traditions of the Stone-Campbell restoration movement and served on executive committees of both the World Convention of Churches of Christ and the European Evangelistic Society. In 1993, Pepperdine University presented him with the

Distinguished Christian Service Award in recognition of his work in "encouraging the reformation and renewal of the church" and his long years as an "enthusiastic promoter of unity and openness in the Stone-Campbell Movement." He continues to publish occasional essays under the title *Soldier On!* These may be found at LeroyGarrett.org, along with most of his other writings.

Bob D. Lewis

SCMePrints@stone-campbell.org
SCM *e*-Prints

Chapter 1:
Confess That We Have Been Wrong About Some Things

Even if we do not hear it as much these days, *What Must One Do to Be Saved?* has long been a favorite "big meeting" sermon among our people, and rightly so, for it is a question right out of the Bible. In giving that title a twist and asking what the Church of Christ itself must do to be saved I am not of course referring to the personal salvation of its individual members. Surely many of the most faithful Christians in the world are in the Church of Christ, and I am not in this article questioning in the least the genuineness of their faith.

I am rather asking what the Church of Christ as a church or as a denomination, if that term is allowed, must do in order to be "saved" as a viable witness to the Christian faith in today's world. What must it do to escape extinction in the decades ahead, or if not extinction, relegated to an insignificant southern or Tennessee-Texas sect? What must it do to save its own people from boredom, mediocrity, and irrelevance? What must it do to escape from its legalistic, sectarian, and isolationist past (if indeed this is a correct assessment) and become a meaningful part of the larger Christian world? What must it do to be true to the Bible and to its own heritage in the Stone-Campbell unity movement, and yet move out on the growing edge toward being truly ecumenical, truly catholic, truly holy, and truly apostolic?

I speak as part of the Church of Christ when I ask what we must do to be liberated from our depressing self-service to being joyous servants of others for Jesus' sake?

Some will doubtless insist that there is nothing to do and that my question is both inappropriate and offensive. I would urge such ones to realize that when it comes to "being what the church ought to be" in the world we have not made much of an impact. Who pays any attention to us? Who listens to us? In what ways have we made any real difference in our world? Not only are we not growing but we have actually decreased in members by the tens of thousands in recent decades. Our typical service is sterile, routine, and boring. Many if not most go to church more out of duty than out of joyous expectation. Our young men are going into business rather than into the ministry. Foreign missions are on the decline. The most revealing sign of all is that too few of our people are joyous, fruit-bearing Christians. Some of our more candid leaders concede that we are dying on the vine.

Others may respond to this by saying that these things are true of other churches as well as of us. That may be true, and it might also be said that as far as the West is concerned we are now in the post-Christian era, that where Christianity was once strong it is now dying. A new Christian age may emerge again in Asia and Africa, but it is dead or dying in the West.

My answer to that is that each church must endeavor to save itself from decadence. I am concerned for Churches of Christ. There are others working for renewal among the Presbyterians, Methodists, Episcopalians, and all the rest, and I wish them well. The best way for us to save each other and become the one Body of Christ together is for each to save itself. We can help all other churches to become more like what God wants them to be by becoming what God wants us to be. I like the prayer of the Chinese Christian who prayed, "Renew your church, O God, beginning with me."

Moreover, I am persuaded that we in Churches of Christ have been guilty in ways that most other churches have not. We have all sinned and fallen short of the glory of God, true, but some of our sins in Churches of Christ have been particularly grievous, and it is these that we must overcome if we are to be saved.

In this first installment I will mention one of the most important things that we must do without delay.

We must confess that we have been wrong about some things.

This should begin in our own assemblies and among our own people. From them it will reach out to others. We must first show some tough love among ourselves, including soul-searching repentance as a people. It will be wonderfully liberating when we can honestly say, "We have been wrong," and in the long pull it will be encouraging to our people and will give them hope of our eventually becoming a more responsible and spiritual people. It will also gain us the respect of our neighbors. I know, for I have seen it work when in visiting other churches I have occasion to confess that we in the Church of Christ have often had a wrong attitude. It always impresses those that are at first critical, especially when one from the Church of Christ is in their service as a visitor, which itself is shock enough!

The sin that we must confess is our patent refusal to have anything to do with other churches and other Christians. In the old days we attacked other churches from the pulpit and mailed out tracts condemning "denominationalism," implying of course that we were not a denomination. On the radio we "skinned the sects" and we debated anyone who had the nerve to take us on. We soon gained the reputation of believing that we were the only true church, the only faithful Christians, and the only ones going to heaven. We succeeded in causing other believers to resent us if not hate us. When they showed such resentment our response was that they didn't really want the truth. In rejecting us they rejected God himself!

In recent years this "skin the sects" attitude has declined. We are now more mature, better educated, wealthier, and more responsible. Sociologists would say we are moving from sect-type church to a denomination-type, which is typical of religious bodies our age. But we are almost as sectarian and exclusivistic as we have ever been. We are now more subtle, more benign in our sectarianism. These days we may not talk about other churches and believers the way we once did, but we still have nothing to do with them. It is as if other churches did not even exist. If it is a joint Thanksgiving or Easter service, no matter how glorious a service it may be, you can count on the Church of Christ having nothing to do with it. Even if it is a joint community effort involving all the churches, such as a campaign to help the homeless, we will not be in on it. It is now common knowledge that if the Church of Christ does anything it does it alone. The Church of Christ has nothing to do with other churches and other Christians (period!).

I am thankful that I can tell people in other churches that this has begun to change. We have numerous churches that are breaking out of this debilitating sectarian syndrome, but they are still far too few, and they are often labeled as "liberal" by the others. About fifty of our congregations pull an "E" in our directory of churches, while many more are moving in that direction. The "E" stands for ecumenical, still a bad word among us even if it is eminently biblical. If we are to be saved these avant garde churches must greatly multiply.

The exclusivism I refer to is evident in our party lingo. Everyone understands that "the Lord's people" or "the Lord's church" refers only to Church of Christ folk. If one of our girls marries a Baptist she is supposed to understand that he is not "a member of the church" even when she considers him a faithful Christian.

We can be saved from such sectarian exclusivism without compromising any truth we hold. Our preachers can belong to the ministerial alliance and we can join "the denominations" in a Thanksgiving service without approving of any doctrine we consider false, just as we can read a commentary written by a Methodist (as we do) or sing hymns written by Roman Catholics (as we do) without approving of any error practiced by those churches.

How can we be the salt of the earth and the light of the world when we have nothing to do with anyone else? Our people spend all their lives in our congregations without ever having heard a minister from another church in one of our pulpits. Most of our people never attend any service of any other church unless it be a funeral or a wedding. We are supposed to be a people who believe in and work for the unity of all Christians — that is our heritage! — but how can we be a witness for the oneness of all believers when we isolate ourselves from all other believers?

There is only one answer to all this: We must change our ways and confess that we have been wrong. We are wrong when we imply that we are the only true church or that we are the only Christians. We are wrong when we suggest that people have to belong to what we call the "Church of Christ" to be saved and go to heaven. We are grievously wrong when we believe that if people are "not of us" they are going to hell.

In order to believe that we are right we do not have to believe that everyone else is wrong. Jesus warned his disciples against a self-righteousness that assumes that if others are "not of us" they cannot be doing the work of God (Mk. 9:38-39). Our own pioneers never thought of themselves as the only Christians and the only true church, forging the motto, "We are not the only Christians, but Christians only."

Our preachers and elders need to say it before our assemblies, *We have been wrong!* I am positive it will have a revolutionary effect for good. There is nothing we could do that would be more liberating for our people. And our leadership would be surprised as to how many would say they never believed that way anyhow!

While we are at it we must confess that we have also been wrong about instrumental music. I concede that this will be hard for us to say, but it must be said if we are to be saved. In coming clean of our partyism we must strip off what we are so widely noted for — not so much our good works but that we believe it is a sin to use instrumental music.

And that is what we must confess, not that we sing acappella, which of course is all right, but in naming something a sin that the Bible does not name a sin, and for making the use of an instrument a test of Christian fellowship. We have something like 3,000,000 sisters and brothers in the Christian Churches/Disciples of Christ who share our heritage, who are "Christians only" and who have been baptized just as we have, but whom we reject because they use instrumental music.

This is our sin, and this we must correct if we are to be saved. We must make it plain that while we choose to sing acappella it is a matter for each church to decide for itself, and that we will no longer condemn others when they differ with us on this and we will no longer make it a test of fellowship. Some of our people can even say that for *them* it would be a sin to have an instrument in that it would violate their conscience. That too is OK so long as they do not impose their opinion on others, making a law where God has not made one.

But again our leaders will find when they at last announce that they will no longer condemn others because of instrumental music that most of our people never believed in doing that in the first place, especially our younger people. Only recently in a large Dallas area Church of Christ a class of sixty young marrieds were asked by the teacher for a show of hands of those who found instrumental music to be a problem. Only a few raised their hand. Several surveys in recent years reveal that among the rank and file of our people instrumental music is a non-issue. And yet it is one of the main reasons why we have been stereotyped as sectarian and antiquated in the eyes of the world.

We have been wrong about some things! It would be a glorious proclamation, and it would cause folk to pay more attention to the important things we are right about.

Chapter 2:
Repent of our petty, narrow sectarianism

I made it clear in the first installment of this series that I am not questioning the personal faith of its members when I speak of what the Churches of Christ must do to be saved. I may even be prejudiced in favor of our people, for I believe they are among the most wonderful Christians in the world, and that is based upon contact with thousands of people in Churches of Christ. When I speak of what we must do to be saved I am referring to our witness as a church in a troubled world that needs us so badly, to our effectiveness as a people of God. If we are "saved" in this sense there are some major changes that we need to make. That is what this series is about.

I may have a quarrel with my own folk in Churches of Christ, but no one can justly accuse me of being vindictive or disloyal. If it is a quarrel, it is a lover's quarrel. I compliment myself only in one respect — I am among the best friends that the Churches of Christ have. I recall reading somewhere that a person who is pleading for change among his own people is paying them a great compliment, for it means that he believes in them and is persuaded that they are capable of greater things.

And I won't leave, never. I feel the same way toward the Church of Christ as I do toward my wife Ouida. To leave her is unthinkable. I assure her that I will stay with her no matter what comes. If she ends up in a wheel chair, I will be at her side. When I was at Princeton Seminary it was suggested that I might become a Presbyterian. No way. The Church of Christ is stuck with me. If they should kick me out, which hasn't happened yet — except that a group of black preachers once withdrew from me along with one of their own "liberal" ministers that I defended, but afterward they rescinded their action — I would be back the next day trying to get in.

Like old Raccoon John Smith, one of our pioneer preachers, used to say to the Baptists when they tried to run him off, I say to the Church of Christ, "I love you too much to leave you!" But as long as I am around I will persistently and lovingly plead with our people to go up higher.

The basis of my quarrel is our parochial, sectarian view of the church. I want our people to think big — ecumenically — when they think of "the church," for this is the biblical view. I want them to envision the Church of Christ as consisting of all those everywhere, all around the world, who sincerely follow Jesus Christ.

We can never be saved for a meaningful and viable ministry to the world and to the church at large so long as we think of "the Church of Christ" in terms of those listed under that name in the Yellow Pages. It is typical for our folk to think of "the church" in a city like Denton, Texas to be only those that have "Church of Christ" on the sign out front. Nobody else. And we limit "the Lord's people" to our own "Church of Christ" folk. The tragedy of this is compounded by the fact that many of our people really believe this. We are the only Christians!

I was reminded of this fallacy on our part when I recently visited the Word of Faith in Farmers Branch (between Denton and Dallas), which bills itself as "Charismatic-Fundamental," where Robert Tilton holds forth. I was there to hear and to see again my friend and brother Pat Boone, who was special guest that Sunday. I had already broken bread that Lord's day with the Singing Oaks Church of Christ in Denton at our 8 a.m. assembly. Two hours later I joined about 4,000 others at Word of Faith, where they really give visitors "the treatment." They make one really feel welcome! At one point in the service I had a crowd of folk around me assuring me that my visit was appreciated. Scores of other visitors were being treated the same way. I was pinned, labeled, given literature and even a free gift (a cassette tape of a previous service).

And they really rev it up — a band (far too loud from where I sat), cheer leaders with pompons, special lighting, multiple song leaders, clapping and stylistic body movements, lots of praising ("Praise Him, church, praise Him!"), video screens that come down out of heaven, uniformed ushers galore — all first class, including the elegant edifice. It is a "health-wealth gospel" church and Rev. Tilton is the star performer. And he does perform, down into the aisles. He does indeed talk about Jesus, but there is no way to miss Tilton. His picture is on billboards and in newspapers from Dallas to Denton. He has a video presentation along with his sermon (on three screens that come down out of heaven) that features him in mission stations around the world.

If you join his church you will get rich (or something akin to that) and you are not to forget Rev. Tilton and Word of Faith when the money starts coming in. One does get the impression that those attending were all doing well, including more than a handful of blacks, but we may presume that those that tried it and did not get rich were no longer around.

The service went for two hours. We stood a lot of that time, revving it up and praising God. It got so loud, especially with the band, that at times I had to cover my ears. It was no place for an innocent non-instrument Church of Christ guy like me, but I was a good sport. But I thought they would never get to Pat Boone, who sat on the large stage all that time. And it is a stage, or a performance center with the latest state-of-the-art electronics. Robert Tilton goes first class, you better believe it! And he is not to be upstaged, not even by Pat Boone.

Tilton saved Pat about 20 or 25 minutes at the end, and he was super as he always is. Pat is not only a sweet singer of gospel hymns, but he is humble and projects the One he sings about rather than himself. That was not true of all who performed that morning!

When he gave his testimony between songs he talked about his life in the Church of Christ, including the preaching he did "at a little frame building in Slidell, Texas" when he was attending the University of North Texas in Denton. He told of his days at "a Church of Christ college in Nashville" (David Lipscomb) where he met his wife Shirley, who was the daughter of Red Foley of country music fame. But Shirley was a Southern Baptist, and even though she had been baptized into Christ just as he had, Pat convinced her that she was not a Christian and that she must be baptized again the right way and in the right church.

He explained that the way he saw it back then was that if a church didn't have the right name over the door it just didn't count. His people were the only true Christians, the only right church. Even though Pat expressed appreciation for Church of Christ people and for his heritage ("I learned to love the Book"), he had laid bare our Achilles heel. Most of his audience, being Texans, knew at least one thing about the Church of Christ — that we think we are the only true church and the only ones going to heaven.

Pat did not know, of course, that I or any others from the Church of Christ were in the audience. When I saw him after the service he hugged my neck and apologized with "I hope I didn't sound bitter." He was not bitter, and we both knew that what he had said was true and that there were things he could have said that he didn't, such as he and Shirley being disfellowshipped by the Church of Christ because of their divergent views on the Holy Spirit. His parents in Nashville were treated the same way by the Church of Christ where they were members, as well as his sister in Dyersburg, Tennessee. I am personally acquainted with all these tragic episodes.

The story Pat told to that big church can be repeated a thousand times over by people who have been virtually destroyed by our exclusivism and sectarianism. People who have never been able to win their spouses because of it; couples who have gone elsewhere after giving up hope that things would change; preachers who have either quit or gone to other churches because they could not adjust to it; elders who have quietly exited because they could not conform to it; young people who have given up religion altogether in disgust.

Beside this we have tens of thousands in our congregations that are discouraged and don't know what to do. They are unhappy with the way things are and yet they don't want to leave. We are a people who theoretically abhor partyism, and yet we have allowed ourselves to become one of the most sectarian churches in America today.

I was present at a mainline Church of Christ recently when a visiting minister did something most unusual. Like a clap of thunder out of a clear sky he asked the assembly, "Has it ever bothered you to have to believe that your Methodist and Baptist neighbors are not even Christians?" He waited for a response. A few brave hands were raised, then a few more, and finally hands were up all over the house. Their hesitation was probably due to shock, for our people just aren't encouraged to do that kind of self-examination.

But that is the kind of thing we must start doing if we are to be saved.

We are at heart a magnanimous people, loving and gracious. Our people do not want to be narrow, bigoted sectarians. We have been sold a bill of goods by well-meaning but misguided leaders of the past who have bamboozled us into believing that if we have any fellowship with a Methodist or a Presbyterian then we endorse or approve of all the errors in those religions. If we call on a Baptist minister to address us or lead a prayer in our assembly, then we compromise the truth and approve of all Baptist doctrine!

We don't ask ourselves, "Then how can we sing 'Lead Kindly Light' in church since it was written by John Henry Newman, a Roman Catholic bishop? In singing that hymn do we have to approve of all that we associate with Roman Catholicism?" If we can't have fellowship with folk with whom we differ, then we can't be in fellowship with anyone, not even our own spouses, for we all differ on some things.

To overcome the kind of advertisement Pat Boone gave us in Dallas — he nailed us to a cross of our own making — we are going to have to be up-front, come clean, and proclaim to the world that we have been wrong and we are sorry, and that we don't believe that way anymore. We are going to have to say it from our pulpits, *We have been wrong!* and publish it in our journals far and wide. The schools of preaching and the Christian colleges must explain to our youth how we went wrong and that we are making (or have made) a mid-course correction.

It is not enough to do or to say nothing, or simply to preach more on grace and about Christ. We must repent. We have a serious sin to confess. We have been factious and sectarian, dividing among ourselves again and again. We have hurt a lot of people and confused even more, and we have churches full of people who are discouraged. We must become intolerant and disgusted with our own petty, narrow sectarianism.

We have been wrong! We are not going to be sectarians anymore! We are ceasing our insensitive practice of having nothing to do with other Christians and other churches! Henceforth we are going to treat all Christians as equals, and we will love and receive them even as Christ loves and receives us!

Let us say these things. You'll see hands going up all over the assembly, all across the country and around the world. It will be a time of liberation for our people. It is not too late for us to be saved.

Chapter 3:
Repent of and confess our sin of division

It is most unusual for a denomination to confess that it has been wrong, but that happened recently with the Dutch Reformed Church in South Africa. The moderator of the church went before a multiracial conference and apologized in behalf of his denomination for the sin of apartheid, which the church had justified on theological grounds for over 200 years.

This was as daring as it was noble for South Africa's main denomination. It was a repudiation of the church's historic practice of justifying the separation of races on biblical grounds. *We have been wrong!*, the leaders of the church told their people, and they are now lending their influence to bring an end to the sin of apartheid. As a result of this bold move some have left the church and formed a splinter group known as the Afrikaner Protestant Church, which will continue to defend apartheid on theological grounds. But the majority has stood up for the Dutch church's position, seeing it as mandated by the gospel and in keeping with the spirit of Christ.

It is noteworthy that the leaders of the Dutch Reformed Church did not simply call for more preaching on grace, brotherly love, and equality between Christians of all races. While that might have kept the boat from rocking too much, it would have been a cop out. They saw that action had to be taken and a sinful tradition reversed. So they publicly repudiated the position of their forebears: *We and our fathers have sinned!*

How noble and courageous of the Dutch Reformed Church! Don't you know that what they did pleased God! Their action will do more to correct the evils of apartheid in South Africa than anything else that has happened. There is power in repentance!

In this series about what my own church must do to be saved I am calling upon the leaders of the Churches of Christ to do as that church in South Africa did, to rise up and say *We have been wrong*. In previous installments I have said that we must confess that we have been wrong in our position on instrumental music, which has set us at odds with every other church in Christendom, including the Christian Churches and Disciples of Christ who share our own heritage and believe and practice what we do except for instrumental music.

I have made it clear that I do not mean that we should start using instruments in our worship, for that would violate the conscience of many of our people. But we must confess that we have been wrong in making instrumental music a test of fellowship and for saying it is sinful for others to use instruments. It is of course right and proper that we should sing accappella if that is our preference and conviction, but it is wrong for us to make our position a command of God for all others. We must repent and confess that we have been wrong in rejecting other of God's children because of their use of instrumental music. We have made a law where God has not made one, and this is wrong. Let us say it, loud and clear!

I have also said that if the Church of Christ is to be saved as a viable witnessing community to a lost world it must repent and confess its sin of exclusivism and of projecting itself as the only true church. We have in fact sold ourselves a bill of goods, handed down to us by sectarian leaders of the past who should have known better, that we and we only are "The Church of Christ." Early on in our history, back in the days of Alexander Campbell and Barton Stone, our motto was "We are Christians only, but not the only Christians." That is right on — biblical, defensible, and even unifying — and that is what our pioneers believed. But since we became the first splinter group of the Stone-Campbell unity movement we have repudiated that slogan by claiming to be the only Christians.

There is a big difference between being Christians only and the only Christians. And it is in that difference that we went wrong. Let's say it, *We have been wrong!* If a denomination in South Africa can do it, we can do it. Let's make it clear that we really believe that wherever God has a child we have a sister or a brother. And that brother or sister doesn't have to see everything eye to eye with us for us to accept him or her as an equal in Christ.

In this installment I am adding another thing we must do to be saved as a people with a message and a mission: We must repent of and confess our sin of internal bickering, debating, and dividing into sects and sub sects. In my home state of Texas we have at least 15 or 20 different kinds of Churches of Christ, large and small, that are at such odds with each other that each considers itself the true church and has no fellowship with any of the others. We have a directory of churches entitled *Where The Saints Meet,* published in Austin, Texas, that lists thousands of our congregations in all 50 states.

But it is a shameful spectacle to behold, for in a sincere effort to list all Churches of Christ the editors felt it necessary, the situation being what it is, to identify each segment with a label all its own — except the "mainline" group, which published the list, which is not so labeled! And so we have "PM" Churches of Christ, meaning that they are premillennial; we have "NC" churches, meaning no classes, that is, non-Sunday school; we have "NB," meaning no building; "NI," meaning non-institutional, "Ch," meaning charismatic. Then there is OC, OCa, OCb and OCc, as well as OC+c, which attempts to identify five different sects of the one cup (for the Lord's supper) Churches of Christ, for while they are all one cup they are divided over fermented or unfermented fruit of the vine, breaking of the loaf before serving, classes, and the pastor system.

We must face the fact that this tragic habit of splitting into sects and sub-sects is due largely to a faulty "Restorationist" hermeneutics, which says there is an identifiable pattern for the work and worship of the church which spells out the necessary details, which when adhered to "restores" the true church. Each wing commander sincerely believes he has followed the pattern exactly and has thus restored the true church. This scenario further insists that the other interpretations of the same pattern are false and so their churches are "unfaithful" and cannot be fellowshipped. So, our divisions have no end. Since 1906 when Churches of Christ separated from the Disciples of Christ we have further fragmented at least once each decade. In some cities in the South there are as many as eight or ten "faithful" Churches of Christ, none of which have any fellowship with the others.

A fallacy that accompanies the pattern-blueprint concept is one that makes unity among believers impossible, for it holds that to be united and enjoy fellowship with each other we have to see all these things alike. Oddly enough, the leaders of our factions dismiss "unity in diversity" as a false doctrine, which by definition that is the only kind of unity that is possible since there is no way for everyone to see everything alike. Whether in a marriage, in nature, or in Christ the only kind of unity there is a unity in diversity. True unity finds its center in a common devotion to Jesus Christ. The common life we are to share, which is what fellowship means, is a matter of each member of the Body "holding fast to the Head" in spite of differences. We don't have to agree on everything or practice everything alike in order to love and accept each other as equals in Christ.

To be saved as a people who can be taken seriously we must show a disdain and an intolerance for our ugly divisions. While it helps, we must do more than preach peace, love, and unity. We must repent of our sins of division and confess that we have been wrong. Like that church in South Africa, we would do well to call a convention for the express purpose of confessing our sin of being one of the most divided, sectarian churches in America.

We need to write out a "Proclamation of Repentance" that would say something like, "Whereas, we have sinned against our Lord's prayer for the unity of all his followers by becoming a factious and divided people; and whereas, we have sinned against the mandate of the holy Scriptures and the holy apostles in their plea for unity; and whereas, we have sinned against our own heritage as a unity people; we do hereby confess our sin and ask for each other's forgiveness, the forgiveness of the larger Christian community, and the forgiveness of Almighty God; and we hereby declare that we repudiate our divisive ways, and are resolved to take the following steps to correct the erroneous course taken by our fathers and by ourselves . . ."

Such a proclamation could circulate as a petition among the churches. It would be signed by thousands. Let it at last be read at our lectureships, on college campuses, in the churches, and let it be published in our journals. Let this be followed by a day of prayer and fasting. Let the press carry the news to the world that we are fed up with our divisions, we repudiate them now and forever, and that we are henceforth a unity people once again.

Nothing has to change in regard to our differences. We can have churches that are premillennial and those that are amillennial, along with many that don't even know what millennialism is about. We can have brethren who support the cooperative radio-TV Herald of Truth program and never watch it and those who are opposed to it but never miss it. We can have Sunday school churches and non-Sunday school churches, as well as those who serve the Supper in ways that differ. We don't have to be of one mind on all such issues in order to be one in Christ. In fact, we are already one in Christ. That happened when we were baptized into Christ and received the gift of the Holy Spirit which is what makes us one.

It is therefore a matter of realizing our oneness and repudiating our factionalism. It is a matter of loving and accepting each other even as Christ loves and accept us. It is a matter of obeying holy Scripture: "Receive one another even as Christ has received you, to the glory of God" (Rom. 15:7). This means that we can and do differ on opinions and methods so long as we are united on the basics of the faith

— and we are united on the essentials, which makes workable the trusted old motto, "In essentials, unity; in non-essentials, liberty; in all things, love."

To be saved as a witnessing church we must show the world how we love one another. No more debating and fussing and dividing. Like Thomas Campbell, we must become sick and tired of the whole sectarian mess. We will show our unity by our love, by our love, by our love. Jesus assures us in Jn. 13:35 that this is how the world will know that we are truly his disciples — not by dotting every "I" and crossing every "T" in doctrinal conformity — but by our love one for another.

Are you ready to sign the proclamation?

Chapter 4:
Recover our heritage as a unity movement

In the last installment I observed that if the Churches of Christ are to be saved as a viable witness to our divided and troubled world they must once and for all repudiate their divisive ways. Since separating ourselves from the Disciples of Christ back in the 1890's, a division that was formally recognized in the Census of 1906, we have continued to divide and sub-divide at the rate of at least one new faction each decade.

These divisions sometimes strike home with cruel irony, for brothers in the same family who grew up in the same congregation and went away to the same college and both made preachers find themselves on different sides of "the issue" that is being made a test of fellowship. Family reunions are a problem since the brothers can no longer "fellowship" each other or even speak to each other. Families are thus torn asunder by our inexcusable factions. We have brought pain to ourselves and disgust to our neighbors. Because of our deplorable partyism and all the legalisms that go with it we have for decades been going to church more and enjoying it less. Petty quarrels have taken joy from our religion.

In my last piece I urged that this be corrected by an open repudiation of our divisive ways. We must announce publicly that we have sinned against our Lord's prayer for the unity of his people; that we have been a disgrace to the community of believers by having a half dozen "faithful" Churches of Christ in a single town, none of whom have any fellowship with the others; and that we have tragically failed to show the one sure sign of being Christ's followers, by loving each other even as he has loved us. I say this should be done publicly so as to make our repudiation of our sectarianism and our resolution to follow the ways of peace as broad as our divisions, which have been strewn across the entire spectrum of our presence as a church.

In this installment I want to add that our salvation as a responsible people of God depends on our recovering our heritage as a unity movement among the church at large, a concept that we have well nigh lost sight of. We must rediscover our roots, the implications of which would be a rude awakening to many of our people who don't know who they are, where they came from, or where they are going. We are by and large a cut-flower people, alienated from our past and separated from our history. We are probably as ahistorical or history-less as any denomination that could be named. For our recent leadership to tell us that we are the true, restored church of the New Testament, and that the intervening 2,000 years of history doesn't matter, is a cruel rip-off.

We must first of all recapture the values of our heritage in the Stone-Campbell Movement in the simplest ways, such as reviving the mottoes and axioms of our pioneers, and coming to see what they meant by them. They were able to pack great truths in small capsules and thus fire the imagination of the people. The first lesson we need to learn about the old

mottoes is that they had mostly to do with
unity, such as "In matters of faith, unity; in
matters of opinion, liberty; in all things, love."
The mottoes help us to see that our forebears
had a passion for unity and that the movement
they launched was an effort to unite the
Christians in all the sects.

To introduce you to other mottoes I will
escort you on a visit to the Disciples of Christ
Historical Society in Nashville, which was
created two generations ago to serve Churches
of Christ as well as Christian Churches and
Disciples of Christ by keeping them in touch
with their history. We have been negligent in
drawing upon the rich resources of this
depository of our heritage. We can correct this
in part by the visit that we now begin.

We pause in the courtyard in front of this
beautiful Gothic library to study the cenotaph
that stands as a memorial to the four leading
pioneers of our Movement: Thomas and
Alexander Campbell, Barton Stone, and Walter
Scott. A cenotaph is a memorial honoring a
person who is buried elsewhere, such as the

Lincoln Memorial and the Washington Monument in the District of Columbia. The "tombs" honor these national heroes, but they are buried elsewhere. The cenotaph honoring our pioneers has their likenesses engraved in stone. Under each likeness there is cut in stone a motto or slogan that epitomizes what his ministry was about. We will study two of these.

Below the stern likeness of Thomas Campbell is the most quoted line in our history outside the Bible itself: "The Church of Christ upon earth is essentially, intentionally, and constitutionally one." This is taken from his *Declaration and Address*, the most famous document of our heritage, being an angry denunciation of division among Christians and a call for the unity of all God's people. Campbell wrote those words in 1809, two years before he started his first congregation known as a "Church of Christ." And yet he wrote of "the Church of Christ upon earth" as if it already existed. This shows that he had no such mentality that Christ's church did not even exist and that he was about to "restore" it according to some recognizable New Testament pattern.

Campbell believed that the church of Jesus Christ not only then existed but that "the gates of Hades" had not prevailed against it since the day of Pentecost when the Holy Spirit breathed it into existence. It was nonetheless in need of renewal or reformation, and that was his mission, especially in terms of restoring love, unity, and fellowship to the church now tragically torn asunder by partyism.

In this insightful statement, capsuled in a single line, Thomas Campbell bequeaths to us the one important truth about the church that we must recapture in our time if we are to find our roots: *The Body of Christ upon earth has existed all through the centuries and it has always by its very nature been one.* Along with Campbell and the apostle Paul we must ask ourselves, "Is Christ divided?" We can't unite the Church of Jesus Christ. It is already one — essentially, intentionally, and constitutionally. This is because the church's unity is a gift of the Holy Spirit to be received.

The church's unity is real but not realized, something like a marriage in trouble. Schisms have imposed themselves upon that unity and obscured it. This is how Campbell viewed his mission, to discover principles of unity and fellowship whereby the church's essential oneness could be realized. It is noteworthy that the passage of Scripture he turned to again and again in his famous document was Rom. 15:7: "Receive one another, even as Christ has received you, to the glory of God."

That verse set the tone for much of what he had to say. Since we were not perfect when Christ received us, and we certainly were not right about everything, we should receive our sisters and brothers on the same basis. We do not have to see everything alike to be united, for oneness and sameness are not identical. And when we accept each other on the grounds that Christ accepts us it will not be to our own glory, as is the case with partyism, but to the glory of God. We don't need to know much more about unity than that!

Under the engraved likeness of Barton Stone on that cenotaph is his pungent slogan "Let the unity of Christians be our polar star," which is a remarkable take of the Lord's prayer for unity in Jn. 17. Stone understood Jesus to say that only a united church could win a lost world, so unity is essential to the church's mission. The polar star (unity) guides the old ship (the church) on its mission (evangelization of the world). When we keep our eye on the polar star by being a loving and united people we will really be God's redeeming community in the world.

A heartfelt recovery of Stone's slogan with all its implication would turn the Churches of Christ in a different direction. Presently we have no conception of ourselves as a unity people. How can we be when we never associate with other churches in any kind of cooperative effort? We can't so much as join with other churches in an Easter or Thanksgiving program. We have been conned into believing that if we associate with other Christians and other churches that we thereby approve or endorse everything they believe and practice. But that is precisely the point of being united in Christ: We can be one without being the same; we can love and accept without approving and endorsing.

So, the cenotaph in Nashville witnesses to our heritage as a unity movement. *Let Christian unity be our polar star. The Church of Christ upon earth is one.* These are dynamic concepts. If we recover these slogans they will help us to think unity rather than division, and they will lead us to pray more for unity, something that we hardly ever do in our assemblies.

We will not have time for an extended visit in the library and archives. Enough to say that the building houses over 100,000 books, pamphlets, papers, letters about our history. They are about a unity movement that God called into existence in this country almost 200 year ago that we in Churches of Christ are supposed to be a part of. I could take you to numerous books and journals in that library that would confirm that fact. I will give but two examples. Dr. Robert Richardson, Alexander Campbell's longtime associate and personal physician, was, according to Campbell himself, the best interpreter of what the movement was all about. I could show you where he wrote in Campbell's paper, the *Millennial Harbinger*, that "This movement was born with a passion for unity, and unity has been its engrossing theme."

The other example would be William Robinson, a British leader of the movement, whose *What the Churches of Christ Stand For* is respected as one of the best statements of what we are supposed to be as a people. In that book, written in 1926, he lists the six significant contributions to the church at large coming out of the Church of Christ heritage. After naming the place we have given to the Bible, the centrality of Christ, the divine nature of the church, baptism and weekly communion, and an aversion to man-made creeds, he lists "an undying passion it has witnessed to the unity of Christ's church." He says, like Richardson, that it started with a passion for Christian unity, and he added, speaking for the British Churches of Christ, "The passion for Christian unity has never been lost."

A passion for Christian unity! Is that where we are in Churches of Christ today? That is where we must come to if we are to be saved.

Chapter 5:
Have our own Vatican II

In our anti-Roman Catholic fervor through the years we Protestants have insisted that the Roman Catholic Church is impervious to change. Rome never changes, we have charged, perhaps with some justification. But Rome has made some dramatic changes in recent years, especially in their ecumenical council known as Vatican II in 1965. Measured in terms of centuries things happened at Vatican II that were wholly unpredictable and would have shocked the fathers of the church of ages past. Indeed, many were shocked in 1965, and are still shocked, causing some clergy to leave and start independent churches.

The leaders of Vatican II were persuaded after much debate that the Roman Catholic Church would have to make some significant changes if it was to relate to the demands of a 21st-century world. They recognized that the church must change or become irrelevant. They raised the same question about the Roman Church that I am raising about the Churches of Christ in this series: *What must the church do to be saved?*

In this installment of our series I am saying that for the Churches of Christ to be saved they must have their own Vatican II. It is not likely that we can effect change in our thinking and practice any more easily than the Roman Church. While change comes painfully and with difficulty, people can and will change when they see that they must do so to be saved. If Rome changed, so can we. What is remarkable about Vatican II is that it set in motion some of the very changes the Churches of Christ must make. That may be because there are striking similarities between the two churches. A review of the changes wrought by Vatican II will point up what I mean.

The story of Vatican II began with a document called "Declaration of Religious Liberty,"[1] sometimes referred to as "the American document" because it was drawn up by an American Jesuit priest and theologian, John Courtney Murray. It sought to undo the sectarian spirit of an earlier document known as the "Syllabus of Errors," in which the Roman Church is depicted as the guardian of all truth while other Christians are viewed as "erring schismatics." The new document called on the Roman Church to recognize religious freedom for all people, and to create an atmosphere of a free and open search for truth in all its institutions.

Murray's document, which he nursed as a mother over a sick child through all the perils of debate and aggravated opposition, brought the Roman Church into a "consciousness of civilized mankind," as Murray put it, and it made the church more accepting of "historical consciousness." These are insights every Protestant church must gain, certainly Churches of Christ who have a way of ignoring history. For the Roman Church to resolve to be a defender of the cause of freedom, religious as well as political, was a change of staggering import.

But Murray's document called for specific changes in thought and practice that were after much controversy approved by the council and by the Pope. To recount these will serve to point up some mid-course changes that we should consider making.

1. *Doctrine does develop; dogma does change.*

We may have as much difficulty admitting this as did the fathers of Vatican II who were as steeped in tradition as ourselves. Murray did not mean, of course, that basic and essential doctrines of the Christian faith change, but that in the general teachings of the church on how to live in a changing world dogma may have to be revised. That the apostles would impose an order or procedure upon the ancient church does not necessarily mean that they would say the same thing to the 21st century church.

In Churches of Christ we need to ask some hard questions about our unchanging practice of male-dominated services, the subjugation of women in ministry, our position on divorce and remarriage, preacher-centered worship, our attitude toward modern biblical research, our polity and various methods of work, worship, and missions.

Murray and the renewal leaders at Vatican II may have first thought it hopeless that the Roman Church would ever conduct mass in English instead of the old Latin. But it was done, to the consternation of many. Could we make some meaningful changes in the way we celebrate the Lord's supper, such as women presiding and serving? The point is that we must become open to that sort of thing. There is nothing wrong in a church saying, "We once believed that way but we don't believe that way anymore; we once practiced that but we do so no longer."

2. *Coercion in matters of conscience is utterly inappropriate.*

It may surprise you that Roman Catholic authorities at Vatican II supported this resolution: "Truth cannot impose itself except by virtue of its own truth, as it makes its entrance into the mind at once quietly and with power." Sounding more like a Luther or a Campbell than like a Pope, they went on to say in that freedom document, "The exercise of religion, of its very nature, consists before all else in those internal, voluntary and free acts whereby man sets the course of his life directly toward God. No merely human power can either command or prohibit acts of this kind."

If you adjudge this as a welcome change for a church that has often through the centuries dominated by coercive means, you must also grant that we in Churches of Christ have also been coercive. If others have been papacy-dominated and church-dominated, we have been elder-dominated, dogma-dominated, tradition-dominated, editor-dominated. If the Roman Church has its written creeds we have had our unwritten creeds, and unwritten ones can be even more coercive and domineering than written ones.

I dare say we have fired more preachers, missionaries, and college professors for doctrinal infractions than the Pope has defrocked recalcitrant priests in a like period of time. And unlike the Roman church, which quietly moves a dissident priest or professor to another post or merely "silences" him, we shoot our wounded. We leave them stranded in mission fields without support. We fire professors while ignoring the right to due process. Once one is a "liberal" or a "false teacher" he or she has no rights. We shoot those among us that are hurting the most — the divorced, the honest dissenters, the sincere doubters. We bruise and batter those who call for change.

3. *We have at times acted "hardly in accord with the spirit of the Gospel and even opposed to it."*

It is amazing that the authorities at Vatican II would look into their history with a critical eye and concede that in their methods they have sometimes been less than Christian, yea even anti-Christian. In this context they went on record declaring that the church should have no special privilege, but only "that full measure of freedom which her care for the salvation of men requires."

If any church on earth needs to declare to the world that it has often been "hardly in accord with the spirit of the Gospel" and has violated the principles of the very Book it claims to honor, it is the Churches of Christ. While the Roman Church has pilloried the schismatics we have skinned the sects. While we claim to believe in unity, we are the one church in the community that is known to have nothing to do with any other Christians. We are widely known as the people who think they are the only ones going to heaven and the only true Christians. The Roman Catholics in Rome in 1965 looked at themselves and said they had been wrong. Why can't the Churches of Christ do the same? To be saved we must have our own Vatican II.

4. *We extend our hand to all other Christians.*

For centuries the Roman Church labeled other Christians as "erring schismatics," but at Vatican II it went on record as acknowledging all other Christians as true brothers and sisters in Christ. It was especially mindful to reach out to the Eastern Churches (such as the Russian and Greek Orthodox), with whom there has been long centuries of bitter controversy and separation. The Orthodox churches are now seen as part of the universal (catholic) church.

While they were at it Vatican II made peace with the Jews, renouncing the long-standing dogma that all Jews past and present are collectively responsible for the crucifixion of Christ. They conceded that the crucifixion of our Lord cannot be blamed "upon all the Jews then living, without distinction, nor upon the Jews of today," and that the Jews cannot be considered as under some curse. To the contrary, Vatican II said, the Jews are under "God's all-embracing love" as are all people.

The Churches of Christ have been so rejecting of other Christians that they must do more than sign a document and make a proclamation, though that would help. We must do things like invite "denominational preachers" (a term we should quit using since we are all denominational) into our pulpits and joining with other churches in special programs. Our people would love it! This we can do without approving of any doctrine or practice that we believe to be wrong. We would simply be saying that since we all are following the Lord Jesus Christ the best we know how we want to help you and want you to help us to follow Christ more nearly, to know him more clearly, and to love him more dearly.

We must regard all other Christians as our equals, beginning right now. We must join with them and with each other in a new spirit of dialogue and mutual respect, a new freshness in perspective and interpretation. We must summons the courage to confront the problems of our own history. We must modernize the Churches of Christ, liberating ourselves from the mentality of the 1940's, and make our religion relevant to our day and time.

Since 1965 fresh air has been blowing through the Vatican windows in Rome. Things are not quite what they once were. Let fresh air blow through the windows of the Churches of Christ. It would be our Vatican II. We can do it. I don't care if you call it Nashville II.

Chapter 6:
Find out who the real enemy is

We've all heard those sermons on how the church is like an army, and we teach our kids to sing *We're in the Lords Army.* According to this imagery we are all Christian soldiers and Jesus is our Captain. We are to put on "the whole armor of God" which is described in detail in Eph. 6. The warrior's gear is all there: loins girded with truth; a breastplate of righteousness; feet shod with the gospel; the shield of faith; the helmet of salvation; the sword of the Spirit, which is the word of God.

There is no question but what one is well armed for battle when he has on such an armor. The Bible describes such a one as "a good soldier of Jesus Christ" (2 Tim. 2:2). A good soldier is not only properly geared but he has the spirit of a fighter. As Paul looked back over his life he said he had not only kept the faith and finished the race, but "I have fought the good fight" (2 Tim. 4:7).

But who is the enemy? Who is it or what is it that we are to fight?

In this installment I am saying that if the Church of Christ is to be saved it must find out who the real enemy is. One only needs to read our church papers to see that for the most part we are fighting each other. Or if one listens to a lot of our sermons and reads our tracts he may conclude that "the denominations" are the enemy. Or if our argumentative spirit is not satisfied in any other way it is some "straw man" that is the enemy. Then there is the long history of our debates. We started out debating "the sects." When they would no longer debate us we started debating one another.

The lectureship audience at Abilene Christian University for 1991 was reminded of all this in a discourse by Jim Woodroof of Searcy, Arkansas. He tells of Gayle Erwin, author of *The Jesus Style,* being a guest in his home. Since Gayle was "not a member of our movement," as Jim put it, Jim's wife Louine asked him if he had ever known anyone in the Church of Christ before he met them. His answer was yes, but he said no more. There was a long pause. "Well?," asked Louine, pressing him to say more. At last he said, a bit embarrassed, "Well, I wondered, 'What on earth did they put in that water?' Because, every one of you I have ever met had always come up out of the water arguing." Jim added an understatement, "We have not been known as peacemakers." He could have said that we've never known who the real enemy is.

I will be the first to confess that I was some time learning what the Scriptures clearly taught all along, that "We do not wrestle with flesh and blood" (Eph. 6:12). Other people are not the enemy. But I learned from my teachers in Church of Christ colleges that it was the Baptists and Methodists who were the enemy, along with the rest of the denominations. If there was an arch-enemy it was the Roman Catholics, particularly the pope. So, I was well armed for such "wrestling," or so I supposed, having been taught by no less a luminary than

N. B. Hardeman himself, who was president of a college that bore his name.

In those early years brother Hardeman was both my hero and my model, for he was a debater as well as a tabernacle revivalist, probably preaching to more people than any man in the history of the Church of Christ. He both debated and preached before thousands. In his classes we studied his debates, which included skirmishes with Christian Church ministers on instrumental music and with Baptists on baptism and apostasy.

One such book that we studied was the Hardeman-Bogard debate, and with brother Hardeman himself as the teacher I got the distinct impression that our man, who was the true soldier in the contest, got the best of the other guy, who was the enemy. It never occurred to me that Ben Bogard was as much my brother in Christ as was N. B. Hardeman. I sometimes wonder how I would have responded if some wise person, like Hardeman himself, had pointed that out to me.

If N. B. H., as he was often called, had said to us, "Now, boys, you understand that Ben Bogard is also a Christian. We differ on some things, as you can see, but we love and accept each other as brothers in Christ nonetheless." If he had said that and meant it, I might have been confused for a time, but I believe I would have listened — and how liberating that would have been!

If Hardeman could have said, "Boys, maybe this debate should never have been held, for it set us against each other as enemies when in fact we were brothers. The differences may not be all that important after all," I am confident it would have changed my life. It would have also changed brother Hardeman's life!

I recall that it appeared odd to me that Ben Bogard was teaching the same debate book to his students in Arkansas, and he advertised the book with more zeal than did brother Hardeman! And of course at the Baptist school Bogard was the true soldier and Hardeman the enemy!

Our big debates through the years have not been as "our sided" as we suppose, including those that go back to Alexander Campbell himself. I recall one faithful "Campbellite" with a critical eye for distinctions challenging the readers of the Campbell-Rice debate.[2] to place what the two men said on the design of baptism side-by-side and identify any significant difference. Rice was a Presbyterian who did quite well for himself in that debate. You might try it for yourself. You may agree that whatever differences there may have been did not call for a big debate where the contestants confronted each other as adversaries instead of brothers in Christ who "love one another fervently from the heart."

It wasn't long until I myself was debating Baptists, and afterwards with my own people in the Church of Christ. We all donned the armor of God and took in hand the sword of the Spirit, and came out flaying away at the enemy — each other! We didn't know who the real enemy was!

I can't blame my early teachers for all this, for I was responsible to think for myself. I have only myself to blame for the years that I was a sectarian. My teachers in those early days did me far more good than they did harm, and I've always loved them for that. Beside, now and again they pointed in a different direction, if I had only known how to follow through. Brother Hardeman, for example, told us in class one day that he believed that his pious Methodist mother died a Christian and that he expected to see her in heaven. "She followed Christ the best she knew how," he told us.

We preacher boys were not into it enough to ask, "Then, brother Hardeman, all those who are following Christ the best they know how are Christians even if they are mistaken about baptism?" If brother Hardeman could have himself followed through on that and made it clear to us that it is not the Methodists that we were to fight when we departed from the sacred confines of his college, it would have made a difference in the kind of preachers we all became.

I would one day learn that the definition Hardeman gave for a Christian — one who is following Christ the best she knows how — is almost word-for-word the definition Alexander Campbell gave over a century before, and that our pioneers were not confused as to who the enemy is, like we are in the Church of Christ. I came to appreciate that old motto that our pioneers handed down to us, "We are Christians only, but not the only Christians." But at Freed-Hardeman College I learned it the other way, that we in the Church of Christ are the only Christians — except for brother Hardeman's mother! All others are the enemy!

The good news in all this is that not only I but thousands of others in the Church of Christ are discovering who the real enemy is. But we yet have a long way to go.

We are learning who the real enemy is because he has captured our kids with drugs and poisoned their minds with pornography. He gets them drunk and slaughters them on our highways. He kills millions of them before they are ever born. He wrecks their homes and breaks up their marriages. He gets us into wars that should never have been fought. He blights our minds with ignorance, racism, pride, and all sorts of godless philosophies, from New Ageism and Occultism to scientism or consumerism.

Tragedy around the world makes it clear who the enemy is. There is civil war in Afghanistan, mass starvation in Ethiopia and Bangladesh, and terrorism in South Africa. In Yugoslavia Serbs and Croats are fighting each other, in India it is Muslims and Hindus, and in North Ireland it is Catholics and Protestants. In Third World nations most people live below the poverty line and suffer gross inequities. We all have a common enemy, whom Luther described as "armed with cruel hate," who is at work the world over seeking to do us in.

When we recognize our common enemy we can rejoice when he suffers a major defeat as in the demise of atheistic Communism in Russia and Eastern Europe. Millions of Christians were persecuted by the atheistic regime in the

Soviet Union, Bibles were outlawed, and thousands of churches closed. Today we have a Church of Christ in Moscow distributing Bibles and the old Orthodox churches are reopening. But it is Communism that was the enemy, not our sisters and brothers in other churches who had to suffer for their faith.

I am well aware that our enemy, whom Rev. 12:10 describes as "the accuser of our brethren" (and that is not just Church of Christ folk!) is at work among all the churches as well as in all the world. He in fact disguises himself as "an angel of light" and invades our pulpits, board rooms, classrooms, and even the editor's desk. He is pictured in the Bible as a roaring lion seeking to devour whom he may. But let all believers unite their energies and fight "the Adversary," and cease fighting one another.

If we are confused as to who the enemy is and start taking it out on each other, it helps some to realize that our Lord's own disciples had the same problem. They came upon someone who was casting out demons in the name of Christ "who does not follow us," and so they forbade him. When they told Jesus about this, he did not approve of their action, saying to them, "He who is not against us is on our side" (Mk. 9:38-40). The disciples didn't know who the enemy was, but Jesus made it clear for them and for us all. The enemy is anyone or any thing that is against Christ and opposes his work. This does not include other believers who are simply mistaken on some points of doctrine or practice. Such ones often love Jesus more than we do and make great sacrifices to support his cause. They certainly are not against him.

So Jesus tells us what 1 John 4:3 tells us: the enemy is "the spirit of Antichrist," all those people, things, and forces that are against Christ and his church. And we are told that there are many anti-christs in the world (1 Jn. 2:18). So we have plenty of enemies to fight without fighting each other. In fact, once we tangle with the real enemy, such as racial injustice, the party spirit, or drug addiction we are grateful to get all the help we can, even if they are "not of us."

Once we see that we are at war with the anti-christs and not with each other or our neighbors who are "following Christ the best they know how," to quote brother Hardeman again, some great things will begin to happen. Our wrestling is "against principalities, against powers, against the rulers of the darkness of this age, against spiritual hosts of wickedness in the heavenly places" (Eph. 6:12).

When we in Churches of Christ realize the enormity of our warfare, that we are in a crucible with cosmic evil, and overcome the mentality that fellow believers are enemies because they are "not of us," we will be saved for a glorious and fruitful ministry.

Chapter 7:
Resurrect the spirit of
J. W. McGarvey *(Redivivus!)*

In this installment of what the Church of Christ must do to be saved I am doing something different in that I am saying we would do well if we would become more like one of our honored pioneers, J. W. McGarvey. This gentle scholar and preacher, more than any of the pioneers, qualifies as "the Church of Christ pioneer." Thomas and Alexander Campbell, Barton Stone, Walter Scott, and Raccoon John Smith are our pioneers only in a secondary sense, for in their day there was no "Church of Christ" as we know it today.

Back in the time of Campbell and Stone our folk (in the larger sense) wore three names: Disciples of Christ, Christian Church, and Church of Christ. They freely used all three names interchangeably. That alone distinguishes them from the tradition of

Churches of Christ, for we are adamant about using that name only. Any congregation that uses any other name is suspect.

It was only when divisions took their toll in the Stone-Campbell movement that the three names took on sectarian meaning. Today those names point to three different denominations. The oldest and original branch has recently made its name official, The Christian Church (Disciples of Christ), though they still sometimes use Church of Christ also. Then there is the unofficial, undenominational Christian Churches / Churches of Christ, who separated from the Disciples of Christ in recent decades, and are often referred to as Independent Christian Churches. They call themselves Christian Churches and Churches of Christ but not Disciples of Christ (not over their dead body!).

We, the Churches of Christ, are the only one of the three branches that uses that name exclusively. We seem to understand that we did not exist as a separate group back in the days of Campbell and Stone. Like the

Independent Christian Church, we became a separate group by way of division, the first major split in the movement, which began to take form in the 1880's and was clearly manifest by 1906 when the U.S. Census listed us as a separate denomination.

So, if we select a "patriarch" (since we do not have patron saints!) or "our honored pioneer" for the Churches of Christ it would hardly be Campbell or Stone. I nominate J. W. McGarvey. In fact I am naming this installment "J. W. McGarvey Redivivus" in that we might be saved if we will resurrect the spirit of McGarvey and encourage our people to follow him as he followed Christ. If we have an alter ego among the pioneers it would be "Little Mac" as he was called and revered by his students at the College of the Bible in Lexington where he served as both professor and president for 40 years. And McGarvey takes us back to Campbell himself, for he studied at the feet of the reformer at Bethany where he gave the Commencement address in Greek. In later years Campbell remembered

McGarvey as one of his best and most gifted students.

McGarvey is our man for one special reason: He was adamantly opposed to instrumental music and vigorously fought against its introduction into the churches of his time. He was the first to argue that the instrument was a sin, and it was he who gave us our arguments against it, including the "argument from silence." He was always exact, logical, scholarly, and persuasive. He was a giant of a scholar, even if diminutive in stature, to have on our side. When he got through lambasting the instrument, there wasn't much left to say.

He opposed the instrument for decades, and the more he opposed it the more the churches adopted it. He at last quit arguing about it and writing about it, and when he was asked why, he conceded that it was hopeless. But he kept the instrument out of his home congregation, the old Broadway church in Lexington, where he served as both elder and preacher, for decades. It remained a cappella in deference to "Brother McGarvey," But the church did have, with Little Mac's approval, two pianos in the basement for Sunday School all those years. I'll concede that's not exactly "Church of Christ," but McGarvey is still our man. After all, he opposed the instrument "in worship"!

When the Broadway church in 1902 at last tired of placating McGarvey and brought in an organ, the old scholar betook himself to another Christian Church across town that elected to remain a cappella. It was a noble testimonial and very Church of Christ-like. He was at the time the most renowned "Campbellite" in Lexington, if not in all of Kentucky, which was a very Campbellite state, and there he was walking out of the mother church for conscience sake.

But being a famous Campbellite isn't all that McGarvey was at that time, for he had become one of the nation's outstanding conservative scholars, and from his desk at the College of the Bible and in the columns of the *Christian Standard* he had stormed the strongholds of modern biblical criticism as it emanated from Germany and the University of Chicago. He answered all the devious arguments of "the higher critics" with the same severity as he opposed instrumental music, sometimes caricaturing them as dishonest and reprehensible. As a teacher of preachers he stood for a strong Bible-centered curriculum. He urged his students to memorize large portions of the Bible, and it was rumored that he himself knew practically all the Bible by heart. He had no equal when it came to communicating the Bible in simple, vital English.

So, there is a reason why Church of Christ colleges have "J. W. McGarvey scholarships" and why he might be canonized as our special pioneer.

But there is one problem in all this: J. W. McGarvey never belonged to the "Church of Christ"! He remained what he had always been, a Disciple of Christ, a Christian only. The story behind this is all the more reason why I call for J. W. McGarvey Redivivus as one more way to save the Churches of Christ.

When we look at the time McGarvey lived, 1829-1911, we see that he lived in the eye of the storm of the controversy that led to the separation of Churches of Christ, formerly recognized in 1906. It is noteworthy that in spite of his opposition to the organ, he refused to make it a test of fellowship, and when the Churches of Christ finally separated over the organ question, he refused to go along. He believed that the Movement did not have to divide over such differences, that there could be "organ" churches and "non-organ" churches and still maintain fellowship. While he opposed the introduction of instruments, he refused to divide over it.

Even though he left his old home church when it brought in the organ, he did not break fellowship with that church. He still visited and would occasionally preach for them, and that is where his funeral was conducted. In short, McGarvey was not a sectarian or an exclusivist. If the Churches of Christ are to be saved, they must resurrect the spirit of McGarvey. Like him, they can be strong in their convictions, including being non-instrumental, without consigning to hell all those who believe and practice differently. Like McGarvey, the Churches of Christ must not make a capella singing a test of fellowship. Again, like McGarvey, we can even say that *for us* instrumental music would be a sin in that it would violate our conscience to use it in worship, but we must not make it a sin for others. We must allow for honest differences on such issues.

The non-divisive spirit of McGarvey is further seen in his relation to Daniel Sommer and David Lipscomb, the "founding fathers" of the Church of Christ, both Editor Bishops, the former in the North, the latter in the South. In 1889 Sommer advocated an "Address and Declaration" in Sand Creek, Illinois in which he withdrew fellowship from the "innovators" over such departures as instrumental music. The document stated that they would not longer consider such ones as brethren. This was the beginning of the separate Church of

Christ in the North. Sommer wrote in his paper that the Church of Christ would soon be as separate from the Christian Church as the Christian Church is separate from the denominations, and he added, "Hallelujah!"!

Since McGarvey was a celebrated scholar and anti-organ, Sommer courted his support. But McGarvey would have nothing to do with Sommer, for while he opposed the organ he did not believe in being factious over it.

So, what I am saying is that the Churches of Christ followed the wrong pioneer. We followed Sommer into sectarianism and exclusivism when we should have followed McGarvey as he followed Christ, by disagreeing without dividing.

Prof. Robert Hooper of David Lipscomb University, a Church of Christ institution, in his book on David Lipscomb, provides a revealing insight into the relationship between McGarvey and Lipscomb. While Lipscomb was also opposed to the organ, his main concern in the South was the imposition of a missionary society upon the churches, which was as "Northern" as it was unscriptural. Hooper rightly points out that Lipscomb was disturbed that McGarvey, who opposed the organ and held to a strict interpretation of the Bible, was a "society man." How could McGarvey oppose the organ and support the missionary society?, Lipscomb lamented.

It is here that Hooper draws a revealing conclusion: "The one thing dividing them was McGarvey's acceptance of the missionary society and his willingness to fellowship those whom he (Lipscomb) considered to be in error." Whether intended or not, the Lipscomb scholar identified what has been the Achilles' heel of the Churches of Christ all these years: *a misunderstanding of the nature of fellowship.* McGarvey understood that fellowship does not imply endorsement, and that he could enjoy communion with those who were "in error" about some things. Lipscomb did not understand that, for he presumed that if the organ and societies were wrong you could not be in fellowship with those who practiced them. Lipscomb confused fellowship and approval; McGarvey did not.

It disturbed Lipscomb that McGarvey would fellowship "brothers in error," a bromide we have hung on ourselves all these years. McGarvey realized that those were the only ones he had to fellowship, for we are all in error about some things. That is precisely the point of Christian fellowship — that we accept each other as Christ has accepted us (Rom. 15:7), and that includes hang-ups, warts, and errors of all sorts. As Christ accepted us! Were we all free of error and right about everything when Christ in his love and mercy accepted us? How compelling! The Churches of Christ will never be saved until they come to see what Lipscomb could not see but what McGarvey did see.

The Lipscomb and Sommer mentality that we have to break fellowship when we differ on some "issue" like an organ or a society has been our undoing. That is why we not only broke fellowship with the Christian Church a century ago and became a separate church, but that is why we break fellowship with each other, spawning a new sect at the rate of one each decade in our 100 years of existence. We differ over the Sunday School and divide! We differ over communion cups and divide! We differ over church cooperation and divide! We differ over the millennium and divide! On and on it goes. We have been sold a bill of goods by Satan — and by some of our well-meaning forebears.

McGarvey is a flesh and blood example that we can look back to and up to, for in him we can see Christ's concern for unity. Study him as he ministered to a little church outside Lexington for 19 years. While they were well acquainted with his scruples about the organ, they eventually adopted it anyway. But they went right on accepting each other without a hitch. He preached for "organ" churches during most of his long ministry, and he insisted that they not defer to his scruples during his visit. This he did because he understood what the fellowship of the Spirit is about. It transcends differences over secondary matters.

Oh, yes, I might add that McGarvey was not only anti-organ and pro-society, but also anti-plurality of cups for the Lord's supper. He had his scruples, didn't he? But therein is the beauty of the brother. He bore his scruples in peace, though not in silence, in "the fellowship of the Spirit" and refused to divide the Body of Christ over such differences.

J. W. McGarvey Redivivus! If in matters of unity and fellowship the Churches of Christ will be more like McGarvey and less like Sommer and Lipscomb they might be saved from obscurantism, isolationism, sectarianism, and factionalism. They were all three anti-organ, but there was a big difference. In that difference lies our salvation.

Chapter 8:
Reexamine our position on instrumental music

(For this installment on what we in Churches of Christ must do to be saved I want you to read someone else, Bob Shaw, a preacher among us who changed his mind about some things after 25 years. While his subject is instrumental music, a question we are going to have to face with more boldness if we are to be saved, it is the spirit of freedom with which he writes and the change he has made in attitude that is especially impressive. It is his courage to think and to question tradition that points to what the Churches of Christ most need if we are to have a viable witness in our kind of world. If we could learn but one thing from his experience it would be wonderfully liberating: that the Bible does *not* make it clear that instrumental music is a sin. You will notice that he is not asking us to adopt instrumental music, but to cease being sectarian about it. Bob is minister to the non-instrumental Church of Christ in Medicine Hat, Alberta, Canada. — *the Editor*)

I spent the first 25 years or so of my life fighting against instrumental music in worship, believing it to be a matter of faith. Since I saw it as a matter of doctrine, I had no qualms for feeling justified in condemning to hell all who used it. During the last 10 years I have become convinced that instrumental music is a matter of opinion. To some this will make me a "liberal" who is not standing up for the truth. But I have the right to change my mind, and I want to tell you why I changed my mind. It was an honest and open look at our "position" and a diligent search of the Scriptures. Here are some of the things I found:

1. I came to see that all references to singing that we use to defend our position were addressed to the individual Christian and not the assembled church. This means that to be consistent we would have to say that instrumental music would be as wrong at home as at church, a position we do not generally take.

2. I came to question if I could really believe that millions of people will be condemned to

hell for violating a law that is not even found in the books. Can you imagine being arrested, tried, and convicted for breaking a law that does not even exist? And we have to admit that there is no law prohibiting instruments in worship. Is not God a just God?

3. I was forced to conclude that if instrumental music is the sin that we have made it then surely God would have made it clear. It would have required just one more line in the Bible. Does not God make matters of salvation clear?

4. I had to face the fact that while we read the Psalms in our assemblies we skip those that call for the use of instruments in praising God. It is as if these psalms were surgically removed from the Bible! Do these psalms call upon people to do that which is sinful?

5. I had to admit to myself that there are good, honest, and knowledgeable Christians who do not see this issue the way we do. Such ones respect the authority of the Bible as much as we do.

6. I was made to see the fallacy of our position by one event in particular. In an open forum at Freed-Hardeman University one of our better known preachers, Guy N. Woods, was asked if it was all right to have an instrument brought into a church building for a wedding. His answer began with: "Since the Bible clearly teaches that instrumental music in worship is sinful . . ." He went on to advise against it since people might think we approved of it in worship.

I must say honestly and sincerely that the Bible *does not* clearly teach that instrumental music in worship is sinful! That is only our deduction and inference. It does in fact clearly teach that instrumental music is fitting and good and pleasing to God (Ps. 92, 147, 150, etc.).

7. I was further disarmed by the promise that God is going to hand me a harp with which to praise him in heaven (Rev. 15:1-3). If God accepted and even commanded instruments in the Old Testament, condemns them in the New Testament, and then

approved of them again for heavenly worship, we must have a vacillating God, which is an unacceptable conclusion. Nor can I conceive of a merciful, loving God giving me an instrument in heaven after condemning millions of others for using them.

8. I came to realize that the basic problem in all this is distinguishing between matters of faith and matters of opinion. The same argument that condemns instrumental music condemns Sunday schools, vacation Bible schools, multiple cups for the Lord's Supper, four-part harmony, and on and on. Until we realize that these are opinions over which we can agree to differ, we will continue to divide.

My purpose in saying these things is not to impose my conclusions on you. They are my own opinion. I do not want to bind them upon your conscience or make them a test of fellowship. We must not allow opinions to drive a wedge between us.

If all of us in a congregation agreed that it would be helpful to our worship to have instruments, I might be in favor of it. Even though I see instrumental music as a matter of opinion, I might still oppose adopting it, even if it did not violate my conscience. It might be lawful but not expedient.

I would not favor going headlong in adopting instrumental music in a Church of Christ, not in our generation at least. It is right for us to sing a cappella as a matter of personal conviction. It also preserves unity among us. It is our attitude that we must change. Our neighbors resent our unloving, unaccepting, and condemnatory attitude toward those who differ with us, even when they envy our ability to sing. We must come to see a cappella singing as our tradition, the method that is better for us, and not a matter of faith and salvation for everyone else. Unless we do honest, truth-seeking, unity-minded brothers and sisters will continue to leave us.

Why can't we practice what we've been preaching all these years? We've always said we speak where the Bible speaks and are silent where the Bible is silent, but do we practice it?

Let's be the generation that puts our derailed unity movement back on track. Let's be more patient and forbearing. Let's become a people that is known for the way we love one another, and let God be the judge of His own people.

Finally, let us revive the old motto and live by it: "In matters of faith, unity; in matters of opinion, liberty; in all things, love." — *867 14th St. NE, Medicine Hat, Alberta, Canada. T1A5W5*

Chapter 9:
Cease being male-dominated

If the Church of Christ is to have an effective witness going into the 21st century, it must make some changes in reference to the place of women in the church. These changes need not be what most of its members would consider radical changes, such as having women as elders or pulpit ministers, but they must be substantial enough to reflect a change in attitude and practice. If there is a concise way to say it would be *the Church of Christ must cease being male-dominated.* Corporate worship is male-dominated, structures are male-dominated, teaching is male-dominated, decision-making is male-dominated. The over-all attitude is male-dominated.

It is not evident that we really believe, "In Christ there is neither male nor female," as Gal. 3:28 urges upon us. If that truth means anything it means that in the Body of Christ gender is not to be an issue. The Church of Christ must take steps to demonstrate that it really believes that oneness in Christ transcends gender. It means that when a member functions as part of the Body it will not matter what sex that member is, just as it will not matter what race the member is.

I submit a list of suggestions of what can be done immediately to help correct what might well be our most besetting sin, the way we treat our sisters in Christ. These are small steps to take, but they will prove liberating, and they are things we can do at once. Not a one of them would violate any Scripture, and they call only for an end to some of our traditions that have no validity. They are not necessarily listed in order of importance.

1. Let the women make some of the announcements and share in welcoming the visitors. This is an important part of the service in all our congregations, especially on Lord's day morning, but it is always done by men. In doing this they should stand before the congregation, behind the pulpit if need be, just

as the men do. In my 60 years in the Church of Christ I have never seen a woman make the announcements or express a welcome. This is a simple matter. We can start next Sunday. This one change might do wonders, one being the congregation might better listen to the announcements! And visitors might feel more welcome!

2. Let our sisters be used in the "Call to Worship," which many of our churches are now having, or "start the service" in those that do not use that terminology. This part of our Sunday morning service could be greatly enriched, and our women would do it beautifully.

3. Let the women read the Scriptures as part of public worship. This too is hardly ever done in a Church of Christ, but it is a step that could easily be taken, next Sunday. It could be the beginning of our taking the public reading of Scripture more seriously. Through the centuries the church catholic has taken seriously the public reading of the Bible, usually from both Testaments and at every

service. Over and over again the NT urges upon us the public reading of the word of God. When we read the Bible at all it is rather poorly done and is not taken seriously. We would do well to follow "the church year" of selected passages, and thus join other churches in what is being read around the world in all the churches. It would be greatly enhanced if much of this were done by the women, who would be encouraged to prepare the week before for the Sunday readings.

4. Let the sisters be part of those who lead the public prayers. Only those who are gifted in this ministry should be used and not "just anybody as long as it's a male," which is our present practice. Our prayers are often dull, repetitious, sterile, humdrum, and so often they are the same old thing sprinkled with Church of Christ clichés, such as "guide, guard, and direct," "ready recollection," and "if we have been found faithful." For the most part we are uncreative and unimaginative in our prayers. The one who leads seldom praises God and almost never lays bare the soul of the congregation before God. In short, we know

almost nothing about leading God's people in prayer. We should have a prayer committee that meets through the week for prayer about leading prayer the next Sunday. Careful preparation should be made. Taking a congregation before the throne of God should be done with great reverence and seriousness. Let's start improving along these lines by turning some of it over to our sisters. Let a woman chair the prayer committee, and watch our prayers take on new life! Those who would deny a woman a part in "the prayers of the church" need to explain why it is that when we assemble in God's house and address Him as our heavenly Father that only His sons may address Him. We gather at His board and around His hearth but only the boys can talk to Him!

5. Let us use the sisters in the serving of the Supper. And while we are at it we need to scrutinize the tasteless way we do Communion. In our larger churches this part of our service begins with those who serve "lining up down front," usually by marching in from either side or down the aisles. There

they stand, all men or boys, gazing at the rest of us and we gaze back. It is an awkward way to enter into an experience so sacred as the Lord's supper. Again, we need a worship committee to search out more appropriate ways to do Communion, and let an innovative-thinking sister and brother serve as co-chairpersons. We could start by visiting the Presbyterians and Episcopalians and see how they do it. The Episcopalians, for instance, have kneelers, and they break bread on their knees! A Jewish-Christian congregation I attended did not use matzo crackers (Lord, forgive us!), but a loaf of bread that was broken and passed (no plate) among the believers. We mistakenly presume that the Scriptures prescribe unleavened bread. They do not. The record says, "Jesus took bread . . ." He took the bread common to his culture. If it was unleavened it was because that was all there was in the house since it was the Jewish passover. He did not *choose* unleavened bread, and he did not prescribe such. If we do as he did, we would "take bread" common to our culture. When I was in Thailand we "took rice," caked like bread. I would suggest a large, handsome French loaf, for it beautifully represents the one Body of Christ. Let the sisters in on it. They'll find edifying ways to do the Supper.

6. Let the big girls serve as greeters and ushers and let the little girls take up and pass out the cards. Do you realize that a little girl in a Church of Christ grows up among us and never does a single thing? Little boys can pass out the cards but not the little girls. It only shows that we start male-domination early. A girl soon realizes that lines are drawn because "I'm not a boy," even among people who are supposed to believe that in Jesus Christ gender does not matter.

7. We must overcome the mentality that says a woman cannot teach a man. If we hold to this tradition by quoting Scripture, we must realize that the Bible can be quoted both ways on that point. We live in a world where women rule nations, govern states, serve in Congress, preside over large corporations and universities, and work as professors and teachers. They are engineers, judges, doctors,

surgeons, architects, jet pilots, and TV news anchors. But in a Church of Christ a woman who serves as a professor of English at the local university cannot teach a class made up of men and women. She can't even teach a class with a 12-year old boy in it if he happens to have been baptized! We don't deserve to be saved if we do not shrug off such nonsense as that!

8. Let our women share in the decision-making process, including the hiring and firing of all church personnel. This can be done through the makeup of committees where women should serve as chairpersons as well as men. An advisory committee, a sizable one in our larger congregations, could serve the elders in studying problems and recommending solutions. The elders, both out of wisdom and for their own protection, should take seriously the advice of such an advisory council. I can see co-chairpersons of such a committee, one a man and one a woman, reporting to the elders "the mind of the congregation," to use a Quaker expression, on some issue before the church. Wise elders

would be slow to act against the advice of such a group, half of whom should be women. This would distribute decision-making throughout the congregation, which is the way it should be in a democratic society, and it would draw upon the wisdom of our women. When there are congregational business meetings women should lead and be heard from as much as men.

9. We can start now in including women in the diaconate. Numerous references in the NT make it evident that women served as deacons (not deaconesses, no such term in the NT) in the earliest churches. There are encouraging signs that Churches of Christ have begun to consider the role of women as deacons, one being a book published in 1989 by Stephen Sandifer of the Southwest Central Church of Christ in Houston on *Deacons: Male and Female?* with the subtitle "A Study for Churches of Christ." This book not only finds support for female deacons in the NT and early church fathers but from our own pioneers in the Restoration Movement as well. The author concludes that eventually the Churches of

Christ might well have some congregations with no deacons at all, some with only male deacons, and some with deacons male and female, and all the options will have support in the NT and in the history of the church.

These are things we can do now, and we must begin liberating ourselves on this issue or we'll be left behind. One might argue that my position would call for women as public preachers and elders as well as these other ministries. Perhaps so, but we have to be realistic. Let's cross the bridges as we get to them. These are things that we can and must do now. Women elders and evangelists are bridges far down the road, bridges we may never come to.

It is like the Roman Catholic theologian I read lately who insists that the pope in Rome will one day be a woman. There is no doubt about it, he insists. It may be a long time in coming but it will come, he says. Well, the Churches of Christ may one day have women as elders and preachers, but it may be about the same time the Roman Catholics have a woman pope! The Roman Catholics, who have long been male-dominated in their services, have already begun to do a number of the things listed above, including women readers. We too can begin to change, now!

It is not my intention in this installment to deal at length with those passages in Paul that restrict the ministry of women, which are partly the cause of our male-domination, along with hearty doses of tradition and male chauvinism. All through the years we have quoted "Let the women keep silent in the churches," but we have made little effort to harmonize that with "Your sons and your daughters shall prophesy." which comes out of our favorite chapter, Acts 2. We quote "I suffer not a woman to teach or to usurp authority over a man, but to be in silence," but neglect those verses by the same apostle that allows a woman to speak and prophesy so long as she has her head covered.

Along the way we have made little effort to relate such divergence by an appeal to the key passage: "In Christ there is neither male nor female." We have a way of picking and choosing what we want from Scripture, based as much upon our prejudices as our passion for truth.

I have no interest in "explaining away" those verses where Paul orders women to be silent in church. As we say of other things, "He said what he meant and meant what he said." Those to whom he was writing should have heeded what he wrote as an apostle of Christ. The question for us is whether he would say the same thing to the churches of the 21st century. The NT makes no claim to be a detailed guide for all succeeding generations, certainly not on secondary issues. It is generally conceded that changing cultural conditions may effect the way a passage is to be applied.

We have no problem applying the label "Does Not Apply" to numerous things in the NT. The injunction to "Greet one another with a holy kiss" appears five times in the NT. A clear command, but we say that it does not apply to us as it stands. Culture, we say. Our

Lord washed feet as an example to his followers, and accompanied it with a command to do likewise. Both an example and a command, but we do not take it at its face value, even though some Christians do. Culture, we say. The same is true of the woman's head covering and long hair. Even the four "necessary things" decided on by the apostles and the Holy Spirit in Acts 15:28-29 we have no problem ignoring with a clear conscience. Custom, we say. The same with the communal plan in the Jerusalem church of owning everything in common (Acts 4:32). When it comes to "approved example" we pick and choose as we will.

It should not be considered strange, therefore, for one to conclude that the restrictions placed on women in the churches of the first century by the apostle Paul were influenced by social factors that might change in succeeding generations. Paul yielded to other social pressures, such as slavery and racial sensitivities, even though he knew Christ transcended such barriers.

Our key passage in Gal 3:28 not only says there is neither male nor female in Christ, but neither Jew nor Greek and neither slave nor free. And yet Paul instructed slaves to submit to their masters, and he returned a runaway slave to his owner. He also circumcised a half-Jew and shaved his own head and took temple vows in order to satisfy Jewish racial prejudices. And yet he knew that "in Christ" there were no such differences.

It is reasonable to conclude, therefore, that the apostle would enjoin things upon women that would serve to protect the church from undue criticism from outsiders. In Paul's world women were hardly more than chattel property. Their word did not count in a court of law. They did not speak in public, and walked not beside but behind their menfolk. In her own home she did not eat at the same table with men. It was part of the synagogue service that a man would thank God for two things, that he was not a Gentile and he was not a woman.

What Must the Church of Christ Do to Be Saved?

Couple this with the likelihood that when some Christian women realized they were free in Christ they may well have become overly enthusiastic in expressing themselves in church. So Paul laid down some restrictions, but it is a mixed bag. He says "It is shameful for a woman to speak in church" (Shameful before God or in the eyes of the public?), and yet he allows her to both pray and prophesy so long as her head is covered (Would this temper criticism from without?).

To apply this mixed bag, which is unclear at best, to all succeeding generations irrespective of changing customs is a bit much. Paul also says that "nature" teaches that it is a shame for a man to have long hair, but again he must be referring to local prejudices, for throughout history "nature" has taught no such thing. Jesus probably had long hair, and one dear soul by the name of Absalom in the OT had hair so long that it got caught in the branches of a tree!

Again, we must begin and end this question with the apostle's enduring principle, one that was revolutionary in its day: *In Christ there is neither male nor female.* Paul could not or would not fully implement this principle in his own situation, probably because of social pressures. The question for us in our day is whether we can and should fully implement it. In a world where women are increasingly gaining their civil rights and where they serve alongside men in all walks of life it is irresponsible for us to say to them that they can't speak in church.

The final arbiter on such matters is our Lord Jesus Christ. Even the apostle Paul said he is to be followed only as he followed Christ. And we can believe that Paul's "neither male nor female" principle came from Jesus Christ. Who can believe that Jesus, who scorned every social bias that separated people, is pleased with a male-dominated church? He talked openly to women when he wasn't supposed to, socialized with them, accepted service from "many women" (Lk. 8:3) who traveled with him, and even referred to one as "a daughter of Abraham" (Lk. 13:16), an unheard of expression in the male-dominated Jewish world.

The only hint that Jesus, like Paul, might have subordinated woman to man is that he did not choose a woman to be an apostle. But neither did he select a Gentile. His mission was to the Jews first, and the number twelve, no more and no less, was probably because what that number meant to the Jews, the twelve patriarchs, twelve tribes, etc. He was creating a witnessing Jewish community that by circumstance excluded women from the inner apostolic circle. But they were very much a part of his ministry and of his life, private and public. Even prostitutes!

In every generation Scripture must be interpreted in keeping with the Spirit of Christ. If an interpretation relegates women to a subordinate and demeaning role in a world where women are being liberated that interpretation must be suspect, either of being misunderstood or being misapplied to our day and time, for it is contrary to the Spirit of Christ.

It is not too late for the Church of Christ to be saved. Its women will help save it. But they have to be given a chance.

Chapter 10:
Have an assurance of our own salvation

If the Church of Christ is to be saved its members must begin to believe that they are saved. You will see that I am using "saved" in different senses. If the Church of Christ is to have a redemptive role and an effective ministry in our changing world, then its members must have a victorious faith and a joyous assurance that they are a redeemed people, saved by God's grace. I am fearful that this is not the case with the majority of our people. We do not *know* that we are saved. We hope we are. We trust that we are. We work at it. We answer the question, "Are you saved?, with a qualified yes at best, such as "If I am faithful . . ."

Seriously, it is a sad state of affairs. Try it for yourself. Ask a few of our people if they are saved. You should be sincere about it and not be putting them on. You will find an alarming degree of uncertainty, and this from members of longstanding, people who are delightful Christians in so many ways. It is simply that they have no real assurance of their salvation. It is a tragedy of no small proportion. And I know where they are coming from, for I was once as uncertain as they. The by-product of such uncertainty is a lack of joy. One thing Church of Christ people aren't, in spite of many noble qualities, is a joyous people. We have little joy because we have little assurance.

We don't talk like people who are assured of their salvation. We don't sing that way. We don't pray that way. That is why our singing is unexciting, our prayers dull, and our services generally boring. Take a look at our Sunday morning service at most any of our churches. Is it a funeral? Where is the spontaneity? Where is the joyous excitement of being a Christian? Who would seek solace from a troubled world among folk who go at their religion with a yawn and a sigh? Let's face it, for the most part we are lukewarm.

Someone has said a gathering of Christians for worship should be something like the locker room of the winners of a Super Bowl game. That may be an overstatement, for there is a place for subdued quietness in our assemblies. But in that quietness there should be a contagious sense of joy, not unlike an athlete sitting quietly before being crowned for winning the race. That says it, we are winners, all the time we are winners in Christ, and we should feel it and act it. We certainly shouldn't have the demeanor of the *losing* team after a Super Bowl game. Yet many of our people behave just that way, like losers. They are scared to live and afraid to die. Are you saved, are you bound for glory? "I hope so. I'm working at it," they say.

But one can't hope that he is saved. Either one is saved or he isn't. One can't hope for what he already has. The object of hope is always in the future. The believer's hope is in eternal life in heaven.

There is no simple solution to this problem. We can't turn ourselves on as one does a faucet. We can't rev ourselves up by some kind of self-analysis. It is not a matter of calling out the cheerleaders. Nor can we solve it by resorting to what caused the problem to start with — by trying harder! If we are to be saved as a church, we must come to see that we have a fundamental problem. And what is that? Hold on to your seat, for it is a shocker: *We don't really believe in the grace of God.*

While we deny it, we really believe in works-salvation. We are saved by being baptized (exactly the right way, mind you!), by taking Communion regularly (it has to be the right day!), and by studying our Bibles (the doctrine has to be exactly right!) To be saved we have to be "faithful" and "right" about all the things that make us good members. No wonder we are nervous when asked if we are saved! Who can measure up to the standard that we set for each other? We keep trying harder, but we are weary of trying. Occasionally we are on a spiritual high, for we have touched all the bases, but we are often down. We scale six rungs of the ladder of perfection one day, and slide down seven rungs the next.

So, to be saved we must seek a fundamental change in our faith. We must quit trying so hard and start surrendering more. We must slough off our self-reliance and our "Do-it-yourself" religion and rely more on God's faithfulness. We must start believing in the gospel of the grace of God, the basis of which is that salvation is His free gift to us. There is no work that we can perform to attain it. There is no way for us to buy it. We can't be good enough to deserve it. There is no power that can wrest it. It is a gift, a free gift, that is ours only because of God's philanthropy. In short we must come to see what has been in holy Scripture all along: "By grace you have been saved through faith, and that not of yourselves, it is the gift of God, not of works, lest anyone should boast" (Eph. 2:8).

This reliance upon the grace of God rather than ourselves must occur one by one among our people. That is the only way it can reach the congregational level. We must "save ourselves" first, by suing for God's mercy, and in that way we can save our sisters and brothers in the Church of Christ. They must "see the grace of God" (Acts 11:23) in us. We may begin by doing what few Church of Christ folk have ever done, by inviting Jesus into our hearts. Let us make the promise of Rev. 3:20 our very own: "Behold, I stand at the door and knock. If anyone hears My voice and opens the door, I will come in to him and dine with him, and he with Me."

This was written to a church, not to the sinners out in the world, though it would apply to them also. But here Jesus is standing at the door of his own church seeking entrance. The minister doesn't have to open the door, or the elders, or the mission committee. You and I are invited to open the door. Here we have the power for change in the Church of Christ. If you want to effect the change, start by getting on your knees and — even if you have never done it before — invite Jesus into your heart. Ask him as he enters to take away all your self-righteousness, your pride and conceit, your resentment and bitterness. Ask him to make his home in your heart. Tell him that you will take him to work with you, to play, to church. Crown him as the Lord of your life, and then praise and thank God for His goodness and mercy. As Jesus lives in our hearts the fruit of love, joy, and peace will grow and abound. Now you will be able to forgive people that you could not forgive before, for you are now drawing upon his goodness rather than your own. That will be your joy!

Along with inviting Jesus into our hearts, which can be done again and again since he can and will move deeper and deeper into us, we should pray the sinner's prayer (Lk. 18:13), "God, be merciful to me a sinner." It is the prayer that impressed Jesus. The lowly publican was justified or made righteous by that prayer, or the faith that it expressed. It should be our prayer too, for we also are sinners in need of God's grace, always, over and over. We have been too much like the Pharisee who in the same story prayed "God, I thank you that I am not like other men," which was the prayer of an insecure believer. Assurance comes only in approaching the throne of God empty-handed and with a contrite heart.

This is the way that we can know that we are saved, fully assured of our redemption in Christ. We can be as sure as Paul was when he wrote in 2 Tim. 1:9, "He has saved us and called us with a holy calling, not according to our works, but according to His own purpose and grace which was given to us in Christ Jesus before time began," and the apostle goes on in verse 12 to say "I know and I am fully persuaded." We don't have to equivocate. We can be sure, for we are relying upon Him "who is able to keep you from falling, and to present you faultless before the presence of His glory with exceeding joy" (Jude 24).

This in no way compromises the necessity of good works in the life of the believer. There is a context in which we can say as Jas. 2:24 says, "You see then that a man is justified by works, and not by faith only." But no matter how great our works may be we are to be like Paul: "not having my own righteousness, which is from the law, but that which is through faith in Christ, the righteousness which is from God by faith" (Philip. 3:9). In Tit. 3:5 he insists that "not by works of righteousness which we have done, but according to His mercy He saved us." It is in that connection that the apostle refers to baptism as "the washing of regeneration." This shows that baptism is not our "work of righteousness" but the work of God's grace upon us.

Included in Alexander Campbell's view of baptism was that it was a pardon-assuring and pardon-certifying act rather than a pardon-procuring act. That is, we do not "gain" or "procure" salvation by being baptized. It is a passive act. God is doing something to us, it is God's "washing of generation" upon us, an act of His grace. In baptism we have the assurance of pardon and the remission of sins. I can know I am a Christian and saved because "I have been to the river and I have been baptized." Campbell used the illustration of a highway sign. One can know he has crossed into the state of Ohio because the sign says so. Baptism is the "sign" indicating that we are pardoned.

This is the force of 1 Pet. 3:21 where baptism is described as "the answer of a good conscience toward God."

Martin Luther viewed baptism in this light. When the pope was calling him the likes of "that drunken priest in Germany," Luther retorted with, "The pope can't talk about me like that, for I have been baptized just as he has." Luther was a good Campbellite! He had assurance of his salvation because he had been baptized. Lest the modern church forget, baptism is an ordinance of God. And what is its purpose? Part of its purpose is to give us something to submit to so that we can know that we have entered into a new state and a new relationship.

If any people should be vigorously confident of their salvation it is Church of Christ folk. And why? Because they have been baptized into Christ. Not baptism in and of itself but all that it signifies, a new life in Christ and a behavior commensurate to that.

Once we see that the only righteousness we can have is Christ's righteousness within us we will have the kind of assurance that is evident in the letter of 1 John. That little apostolic love letter has a way of linking the Christian's assurance with a life of love, as in 1 Jn. 3:14: "We know that we have passed from death to life, because we love the brethren."

We know because we love! When that great truth becomes our own we will be saved as a people. Let it be so!

Chapter 11:
Recognize that we can't be a first century church

Hanging about the neck of the Church of Christ like an albatross all these years has been the fiction that we are the first century church duly restored in name, organization, worship, doctrine, and practice. It is a fiction grounded on false assumptions, such as the church of the apostles having a particular name, which it did not, and that it had a uniform organization and clearly-defined "acts" of worship, which it did not.

But the first thing we must come to terms with if we are to rid ourselves of the weighty albatross is a proposition that can hardly be questioned: *We can't be a first century church!* There is no ground for supposing that God ever intended for His church in each succeeding century for the past 2,000 years to be a first century church, even if it were possible, which it isn't. That one simple fact, duly accepted and acted upon, would go far in saving the Church of Christ, to wit, *that it is impossible to be a first century church in the 21st century.*

The evidence rather suggests that God calls us to do for our generation what the primitive church did for its generation. Nothing in Scripture indicates that the earliest congregations were intended to be models for all time to come or even in their own time for that matter. The facts of history, culture, and civilization demand that the Church of Christ of the second century would be a second century church and that the church of the sixteenth century would be a sixteenth century church. Each generation of Christians is to serve its own time, drawing upon both holy Scripture and the experience of the church through the ages (tradition) for its direction. We have to recognize that time makes a difference in the way Scripture is to be interpreted.

All these years we have suffered from the illusion of a golden age of the church in the past. Historical study has exploded this illusion, for we now know there was never a golden age, not even in the case of the earliest churches which had problems as serious as those of most any other period. We have what one of our pioneer preachers, Walter Scott, called "the golden oracle," which referred to the grand truth that Jesus Christ is the Son of God, but we have had no golden age. The fact that the primitive church had many diverse elements, both Jewish and Gentile, and only gradually emerged from its Jewish context to have a character of its own makes any golden age interpretation impossible. The church has always in every generation been far less than perfect.

We have erred in our claim that there is a uniform pattern of organization and worship in the New Testament churches and that we have duly "restored" that pattern. This is evident in the fact that we can't even agree among ourselves as to what that pattern requires. We have not only differed but divided over almost every aspect of the life of the church, whether it has to do with using instruments of music, missionary and benevolent societies, Sunday schools, the manner of serving Communion, cooperative efforts, work of elders and preachers, etc., etc. Are we to conclude that God has given us a prescribed norm or pattern that is so obscure that we ourselves cannot make head or tail of it? Or is it that we have erred in making the New Testament something that it never has been and was never intended to be?

There are three fallacies that we have succumbed to as a result of presuming that we are to be a first century church in the 21st century. A close look at them may help us to free ourselves from them.

1. *That the silence of Scripture on any proposed new method is equivalent to a denial of its legitimacy.*

It is interesting that Alexander Campbell in his earlier years was misled by this fallacy. When a new method of doing the church's work was proposed to him, he retorted with, "It is not commanded." Experience taught him that the "silence" argument confines the church to centuries past and makes useful innovations impossible. By 1849 Campbell was ready for his congregations to pool their efforts in an organized missionary society and he served as its first president. He was by now asking different questions about a proposed innovation, such as whether it is in harmony with the plain teaching of Scripture, whether it is in keeping with the Spirit of Christ, and whether it will promote the cause of Christ in our age?

Today we live in a Telstar, computerized age, and we can hardly imagine what the next century will bring. But we know that human nature will not change and that because of humankind's fallenness people will always be in need of redemption. That is why we have an unchanging gospel that transcends all time. But means and methods will change, as will traditions and marginal and secondary matters. With the passing of centuries we have learned that many things are legitimate that are not specifically prescribed in Scripture, such as buildings and baptistries. It should not be a question of whether a helpful innovation is prescribed but whether it is proscribed.

2. *That the true church must be an exact copy of the original church in all its details.*

In this proposition, which has had great influence upon Churches of Christ, there is more than one fallacy. The first is the fiction that there is such a thing as "the true church," if one means by that a church that is right about everything. There has never been such a church, including the ones set up by the apostles. One only needs to read about the congregations in the New Testament to see how imperfect they were.

The second false premise is that the "the original church" can be identified with such detail that an exact copy can be produced in succeeding centuries. Not all that many details are known and they differ from church to church. And even if the exact details could be ascertained, are we sure we should follow all of them? Do we want to be an exact copy of the Church of Christ in Jerusalem where each member sold his and her possessions and resorted to communal living? Or the church in Corinth where some believed in "lords many and gods many," where there were factions, and where they even practiced pagan rites in being baptized for the dead? If we sought to be like the church at Pergamus we could probably do without the doctrine of the Nicolaitans, whatever that was. And we wouldn't want to be "wretched, miserable, poor, blind, and naked" like the congregation at Laodicea.

When theologian Karl Barth was asked about how to identify a true church, he said that a true church is where the power of Christ is present in the lives of the people. That is a better answer than the illusion that we are "an exact copy" of some "original pattern" that never existed to begin with.

3. *The demand for book, chapter and verse for what is only improvements in modern culture.*

The church should be the first to make use of the modern technology that has given us a world of instant communication. Fax machines and computers now do what would have appeared miraculous only a few years back, and we travel about the world at incredible speed. The church is to capture such a world for Christ rather than to isolate itself into a first century (or even a 1940's) mentality. We must not allow ourselves to be held back by those who demand book, chapter and verse for the use of an overhead projector or any other means, great or small, that furthers the cause of Christ.

I belong to a Church of Christ that not only has duplicating machines and computers but a workroom with all sorts of gadgets and teaching aids, spacious offices and reception rooms, a family activity center (with kitchen, stage, basketball court, etc.), a gazebo out in the garden, a prayer room, etc. Committees oversee mission projects at home and abroad, Meals on Wheels, campus ministry, youth ministry, and many more. Imagine a Church of Christ with a prayer room and a prayer ministry, with call-in recorders and all the rest! One thing is sure, we are not a first century church! The paved parking lot with hundreds of high-powered automobiles makes that evident.

Our response to the demand for a changing church in a changing world should be a blend of common sense and vital piety, which does not call for a Bible verse for every modern innovation. The question ought to be whether all such things are in keeping with the Spirit of Christ, whether they are a proper use of financial resources, and whether they are used to the glory of God. The rule should be to use things and love people, not the other way around. That means we will use such things in order to be a servant church rather than a self-serving church. So, the church of every age since apostolic times should say to the world around it, "We are your servants for Jesus' sake," but ways of doing this will change.

What then is "the pattern" for the church of the 21st century. Ever since the light shined in the darkness and the darkness could not apprehend it the pattern for God's community on earth has been the same, Jesus Christ our Lord. According to 2 Cor. 3:18 it is his image that we behold as in a mirror, and it is his likeness that we, his church, are being conformed to, from one level of glory to another, and this by the Holy Spirit within us. Jesus Christ is the church's pattern, and to the extent that the Bible shows us how to take on his likeness it may be referred to as our pattern. The Bible is our guide in that it reveals Jesus Christ.

We are thus to take the Scriptures in hand in order to see Jesus, for "they testify of me," as Jesus himself put it in Jn. 5:39. That verse teaches us that we are not to be like the Pharisees who supposed that in the Scriptures themselves they had eternal life. If we liken the Bible to a telescope we are not to be like a monkey that looks *at* the telescope, but we are to look *through* the telescope in order to see the Person who is our pattern.

No one congregation in the New Testament therefore can be viewed as our pattern, nor all of them together, but out of their experiences, their strengths and weaknesses, we learn how to be his church. Out of the documents that we call the New Testament "the essentials" of the faith emerge and they become our norm for all generations, for it is the essentials that point us to Christ.

The gospel of the grace of God is forever, as are the ordinances of that gospel. Means, methods, and secondary matters, which are effected by cultural change, will vary with the generations. This calls for a responsible handling of Scripture by the church of every age lest we cling to the Book itself and lose sight of the Person.

Chapter 12:
Abandon our claim to exclusive truth

There is a liberating truth that would go far in saving the Church of Christ from the obscurant course it has followed during the century of its existence: *We can believe we are right without having to believe that everyone else is wrong.* For one hundred years, ever since it was bequeathed to us by well-meaning but misguided leaders at Sand Creek, Illinois in 1889, the Church of Christ has been hamstrung by the fallacy that if we surrender our claim to exclusive truth we forfeit our right to exist. If we are right, everyone else has to be wrong. Not so. If we are true and faithful Christians, then no one else is. That does not follow. Our *raison d'etre* depends upon our being the one and only true church. Wrong again. We have been sold a bill of goods by those who would make us a fissiparous sect forever engaged in the "jarrings and janglings of sectarian strife," to quote Thomas Campbell.

We must first of all realize that this claim to exclusive truth was not the position held by the pioneers of the Restoration Movement. They launched "a movement to unite the Christians in all the sects," a goal that clearly implied that there were Christians in the sects. One of their mottoes was, "We are Christians only but not the only Christians." It was never their claim that they were the only Christians, the only true church, and they were not exclusivists. Alexander Campbell left the Presbyterians and was "forced out" (as he saw it) by the Baptists, but he never broke fellowship with either and always considered them Christians. In his reply to a question in the often-quoted Lunenburg Letter he said if there were no Christians in the sects there were none anywhere.

It is a little known fact that the first congregations of the Campbell movement, Brush Run and Wellsburg (both in Virginia near Bethany, Campbell's home) were members of a Baptist association of churches, the first the Redstone association, the second the Mahoning association. A third congregation in Pittsburg, led by Thomas Campbell, sought membership in a Presbyterian presbytery and was turned down. Alexander Campbell frequently spoke for various denominations, and their clergy were often visitors in his home and spoke at the college he founded on his own farm. When he went to Nashville to oppose Jesse Ferguson, the Church of Christ minister who was conducting séances with the dead, he first spoke at the Methodist church where he was introduced by the bishop who offered support for the difficult task he had in their city.

All this stands in bold contrast to the Church of Christ today where a preacher is suspect if he has any such contact with other believers. For example, Bill Banowsky, a prominent Church of Christ minister, has in recent years been guest speaker at various denominations. He told a class at the Highland Oaks Church of Christ in Dallas, in a splendid lesson on unity that I heard on tape, that he had been criticized more for his visits to other churches than anything else he had ever done, and he added that he had done a lot of shady things. When the elders of a church in south Texas heard that brother Banowsky had preached for a Methodist church, they cancelled the appointment he had at their church.

This is by no means atypical among Churches of Christ. All these years it has been an accepted fact that whatever cooperative effort the churches in a town may promote they cannot count on the Church of Christ helping out. It is rare for a Church of Christ minister to participate in the ministerial association, and if he takes part in a city-wide Easter or Thanksgiving service he does so at his own risk. A person may spend a lifetime in a Church of Christ without ever hearing anyone from any other church, and except for weddings and funerals never visit any other church. We have no fellowship with other churches and other Christians (period).

And yet we claim to be a unity-minded people and heirs of a unity movement. How can we have an effective unity plea when we have nothing to do with anyone else?

Not only is our exclusivism at odds with our own heritage in the Stone-Campbell movement, it is also contrary to the teaching of Christ, who was not an exclusivist. And he taught his disciples that they were not to be absolutists. Mark 9:38-40 tells how one of the disciples said to Jesus, "Teacher, we saw someone who does not follow us casting out demons in Your name, and we forbade him because he does not follow us." It was one of those things that pride often dictates — if someone is not "of us" he does not count. This was the ideal time for Jesus to call for a narrow view if such was his intention.

His response must have startled the disciples who by then supposed they had the exclusive claim to truth and the only ones qualified to teach it. "Do not forbid him," Jesus told them "for no one who works a miracle in My name can soon afterward speak evil of

Me." He went on to speak a truth we are slow to learn: "He who is not against us is on our side." We might be surprised how many there are that Jesus would accept as on his side.

It is one thing for us to believe in absolute truth, which we all do since we believe in God, but it is something much different for us to presume that we have an absolute understanding of that truth. Truth is absolute, our grasp of truth is relative. One sobering truth speaks to that: "For now we see in a mirror, dimly, but then face to face. Now I know in part, but then I shall know just as I also am known" (1 Cor. 13:12). So, we can surrender our claim to exclusive truth (only we have all the truth) and still believe in absolute truth (which is a reality that is beyond our perfect understanding).

On the face of it, we are forced to conclude that we *must* abandon our claim to exclusive truth in order to be an authentic people. We have no right to exist believing that we and we only have the truth. We must admit that we are both fallible and finite, that we, like everyone else, are wrong about some things and ignorant about other things. We must include ourselves in Alexander Pope's wise dictum: "To err is human, to forgive is divine." The Bible mandates that we acknowledge our ignorance: "If anyone thinks that he knows anything, he knows nothing yet as he ought to know" (1 Cor.8:2). The next verse shows that what is really important is not whether we know God but whether he knows us!

And yet we can believe, in common with all Christians, that we have found many precious truths that we live for and would die for. It is not so much that we *know* certain truth, for "Knowledge puffs up while love builds up," but that we *believe* that truth and act upon it in love. We are not saved by knowledge but by faith that works by love.

There are some compelling reasons why the Church of Christ must abandon its claim to exclusive truth:

1. *Such a claim is seen by others as rude, arrogant, and self-righteous, and it hinders people from hearing us with an open mind.*

Fair-minded people understandably resent those who believe they are right and everyone else is wrong. All through the years we have been accused of believing we are the only ones going to heaven, that we are the only Christians and the only true church. This is not only rude and arrogant but nonsense, for the Church of Christ, counting all its factions, comprise less than one-tenth of one percent of the hundreds of millions that make up the Christian world. Furthermore, such a view dechristianizes many of the noblest, most dedicated believers who have sacrificed for the cause of Christ more than ourselves.

2. *Such a claim makes us look ridiculously inconsistent when we draw upon the labors of other Christians and yet say they are not Christians.*

We sing the great hymns of Martin Luther ("A Mighty Fortress Is Our God"), John Henry Newman, who was a Roman Catholic bishop

("Lead, Kindly Light"), and Charles Wesley, one of the founders of Methodism ("I know That My Redeemer Lives"). We use translations of the Bible produced through the centuries by the church at large. We study the commentaries and read the books of scholars that do not even know about the Church of Christ. We send our missionaries to the language schools of the various denominations and our college professors are educated at seminaries and universities of various churches. This is "taxation without salvation"!

3. Such a claim contradicts the Bible in that it implies that Christ had no church upon the earth and that there were no Christians during most of the past two thousand years.

It is disarming to our people when they realize that what they call "the Church of Christ" is only a century old, and the Restoration Movement out of which it emerged is only two centuries old. Our claim to exclusive truth cancels 1900 years of history: no church, no Christians! Not even William Tyndale who was burned at the stake in 1536

for translating the Bible into English. Our Lord
made it clear that the gates of hell would not
prevail against his church, and we know from
history that his church has always been
around, "living still in spite of dungeon, fire,
and sword." This makes it clear that distinction
must be made between "the Church of Christ
upon earth" that Thomas Campbell talked
about and the Yellow-Pages Church of Christ.

4. *Such a claim makes separatists of the Church
of Christ and makes it impossible for it to be part of
a unity movement.*

There is no way for us to make an effective
plea for unity so long as we assume an
exclusivistic posture. Other believers will
ignore us so long as we refuse to have any
fellowship with them. We can only preach
conformity ("Be like us; we are the true
church!"); we cannot plead for unity ("Let's
join hands and grow closer to Christ together!).
And yet unity is our heritage. We must plead
for unity in diversity, which is the only kind of
unity there is, and for disagreement without
division, which is the only way to "preserve

the unity of the Spirit in the bond of peace," which is a Biblical charge.

5. *Such a claim stands on the false premise that there can be perfect knowledge and perfect obedience.*

This has been our undoing in the Church of Christ. We have to be right about everything, with every *i* dotted and every *t* crossed. We have not come to terms with the grace of God. This is why we can never be sure of our salvation. We try and try harder, but we are never sure. Once we realize that acceptance with God is not a matter of our goodness or our works or our perfect knowledge and obedience, but a matter of surrendering to God's grace, we will abandon our claim to exclusive truth.

The good news in all this is that there are many, perhaps a majority, in the Church of Christ that are already abandoning our claim to exclusive truth. It is the leadership that is hesitant. A growing number are realizing that their *raison d'etre* does not depend upon the naive claim that we have a monopoly upon God's truth.

We have impelling reasons to exist as the Church of Christ, the most significant being that ours is a unity heritage and we are to be busy promoting the cause of the unity of all believers. We are within the tradition of Barton W. Stone whose motto was, "Let Christian unity be our polar star."

Along with being a unity movement, we exist in order to be a productive part of the Body of Christ, filled with the Spirit and bearing its fruit of love, joy, and peace. We exist in order to be an intelligent and responsible community of believers sensitive to the needs of a suffering world. We exist in order to become more and more like Christ by being a servant community. We exist in order to help redeem fallen humanity by being the salt of the earth and the light of the world. And always a pilgrim church, whose home is not in this world, that is living *in* time but *for* eternity.

All this is our *raison d'etre* and it is more meaningful when we see ourselves, not as a church that has exclusive truth, but as a people always in search of truth, especially as it is revealed in Jesus Christ. And always eager to accept other Christians as equals and join with them in the unending search for more and more truth.

Chapter 13:
Come to terms with our status as a denomination

If the Church of Christ is to be saved for a meaningful ministry in the 21st century it must come to terms with its status as a distinct religious body, to wit, that it is at worst a sect, at best a denomination. This is imperative for one vital reason, self-authenticity. If we are to be a redemptive people in a troubled world we must be an honest people. We can't play such games as "They are all denominations (or sects), but we are not" and have any viable impact upon a lost world. Ministers in other churches are "denominational preachers" while ours are "gospel preachers." All other churches are "sectarian churches" while we are "the church." It is understandable that our neighbors not only see this as arrogant, but it causes them to beg to be excused when it comes to having anything to do with us.

A case in point is a seminary professor's review of one of our publications entitled *I Just Want To Be A Christian* by Rubel Shelly. He describes the overall impression the book made on him in these words:

> At first reading I confess to some indignation at his distinction between "the sectarian churches," by which he means everybody else, and "nonsectarian churches," by which he refers to those "streams" that have emerged from the American Restoration Movement. In fact, the mentality is easy enough to understand: it is exactly the same as that found in the Roman Catholic Church.[3]

The professor went on to explain his comparison between Roman Catholics and the Church of Christ:

> Conservative Roman Catholics do not view themselves as a denomination. They think of themselves as the one, true, holy, apostolic church. For them Christian unity does not have to do with getting denominations together, but on returning to the one, true, holy, apostolic church.[3]

He said that this is precisely Shelly's position except that in his case the true fold is the Restoration Movement. The professor goes on to express his astonishment that the Church of Christ could have such "an extraordinarily narrow focus" as to the number of Christians in the world — a view even narrower than conservative Catholics!

The professor could be advised that it is not as bad as he has been led to suppose, for the majority of those in Churches of Christ no longer hold such a narrow view. But they are not being supported by their leaders who continue to parrot the stale party line, "We are not a denomination like all the others." For many years in this journal I have responded to that claim by asking, if we are not a denomination what would we have to have to be a denomination that we don't already have? In one article years ago I stated it in a syllogism:

By definition a denomination is a church with a particular name.

The Church of Christ has a particular name.

Therefore, the Church of Christ is a denomination.

There it is for those who want logic. Case closed.

But there are other recognizable features to a denomination:

It has its own agencies, such as schools, colleges, publishing houses, journals, conventions, missionary programs, retirement plans.

It has its own distinctive clergy, separate from those in other groups.

It has its own definable doctrines.

It has its own history and traditions that set it apart.

It has its own list of churches in a yearbook or directory. (This is considered the one sure sign of a fully developed denomination. Note:

the Bible churches have not yet reached this stage.)

The Church of Christ clearly qualifies on each of these points. So, I ask again of our leaders who keep insisting, even in our more liberating books like Rubel Shelly's, that we are not a denomination: *What would we have to have to be a denomination that we don't already have?*

It might be argued that we are not a denomination because we have no national headquarters, no ecclesiastical hierarchy. But there are many denominations that are congregational in polity and have no ecclesiastical hierarchy.

There is really no contest. Our leaders know that the Church of Christ is a denomination. They just won't admit it! Pardon my candor, but it is a case of not being honest with our people. And that is what we have to do to be saved, be honest and cut out the nonsense.

It is more serious than just nonsense, for we actually abuse the Bible in our resolve to avoid calling ourselves a denomination. We take a beautiful term like fellowship, *koinonia,* which in Scripture refers to all those who are in Christ and in "the fellowship of the Spirit," and use it in a narrow, sectarian sense. We say "Our fellowship" when we refer only to Churches of Christ. A flagrant and inexcusable abuse of Scripture! We do the same thing with "the Lord's church" or "the churches of Christ," Biblical terms indeed, but we apply them to only part of the Body of Christ, ourselves only.

But, considering the state of the religious world, we have to have a name if we prevail as a separate church, and we chose Church of Christ, or Daniel Sommer chose it for us back in 1889 when he wanted to distinguish us from the Disciples of Christ or Christian Churches. I don't know that it is all that bad to have a denominational name, considering that the state of things is not ideal, and "Church of Christ" is a good name, a *denominational* name. I am only saying that we should admit it. Go ahead and say it, "Our denomination." It will do your soul good! That is better than resorting to euphemisms and far better than prostituting Biblical terminology. Of course, you can always say "Our movement," one of our more sophisticated euphemisms. Anything but denomination!

Our aversion to that term is of late vintage, for our pioneers realized early on that they had added one more denomination to the world scene and did not deny it, even if it wasn't their intention at the outset. This line from Alexander Campbell might surprise some of our folk:

> We, as a denomination, are as desirous as ever to unite and cooperate with all Christians on the broad and vital principles of the New and everlasting Covenant (*Mill. Harb.*, 1840, p. 556).

We, as a denomination! Alexander Campbell! We might have to withdraw fellowship from him for that! Note also that he not only recognized that there were Christians in "other denominations" but that he was eager to cooperate with them. This shows that our exclusivism of having no fellowship with other churches is of more recent date than Campbell's time, only the past one hundred years in fact.

But at the same time Campbell was quick to distinguish between a denomination and a sect, insisting that his people were not a sect. In his debate with Mr. Rice, who accused him of starting another sect, he retorted, "You can never make a sect of us," and went on to emphasize the catholic (universal) nature of his plea for the unity of all Christians, such as a catholic name, a catholic baptism, a catholic plea. The distinction between sect and denomination is vital. One reason we've had such a hang up about denominations all these years may be because we have made it equivalent with sect. One is condemned in Scripture, the other is not. A sect presumes to be the whole of the Body of Christ, exclusive of all other believers, while a denomination recognizes that it is only part of the whole. Too, a people can be a denomination as a temporary measure, looking for the time when the ideal will obtain and there will no longer be denominations but only the one Body of Jesus Christ.

While the Church of Christ started as a sect back in 1889 in Sand Creek, Illinois when we rejected as brethren even those in Christian Churches, we are today somewhere on the continuum between sect and denomination. If the Mormons are a sect with some denominational characteristics, I would say the Church of Christ is a denomination with some sectarian characteristics. So, it is a worthy goal to keep on being more denominational and less and less sectarian. Our most sectarian trait is our exclusivism. One way to become less sectarian is to admit that we are a denomination! Those people who call all others "sectarian" are almost certainly sectarian themselves.

"A denomination in protest" is a defensible position. We can even say that we are a denomination because we can't help being, and that we don't believe in denominations as the ideal or the final end for the church, and that we will work for that unity that will one day cause denominations "to die, be dissolved, and sink into union with the Body of Christ at large," to quote another of our founding documents.

I challenge the leadership of the Church of Christ to be as forthright as Mr. Campbell was. Who will be the first to step out and say, "We, as a denomination . . ."? This we can do without surrendering any truth we hold, and it will be an important step toward saving the Church of Christ.

Chapter 14:
Stand in the grace of God

This is the true grace of God in which you stand. — 1 Pet. 5:12

Every member of the Church of Christ believes in the grace of God. They would all readily acknowledge that we are saved by the grace of God and not by our own works. No one among us has the slightest interest in minimizing the significance of the grace of God.

When I say in this installment that if the Church of Christ is to be saved it must, as the above passage indicates, *stand* in the grace of God, and not simply believe in it. The Church of Christ has a head knowledge of grace, but at the gut level it does not, generally, know the grace of God. To put it another way, we must come to terms with the grace of God, recognizing that it is a reality to be realized. It is like living in a house wired for electricity and not being plugged into the power. This is why we're not going anywhere, we're not plugged in.

When we consider what grace does for people, we do not appear to have "seen the grace of God," to quote Acts 11:23, even though we believe it is around. Grace makes believers more and more like Christ, but we are not known for our Christlikeness. Grace causes them to exult in their blessings, filling them with joy, good humor, and laughter; but we are not known for those qualities. Grace makes people gracious, less critical, more tolerant and more accepting; but is this where we are? Grace is never what one deserves, but is this what we have emphasized? Grace is God's free gift, unconditionally bestowed, no strings attached; but haven't we attached strings?

To put all this another way, the Church of Christ may be guilty of doing to the grace of God what Paul took pains not to do, as in Gal. 2:21: "I do not set aside the grace of God, for if righteousness comes through the law, then

Christ died in vain." The RSV has it, "I do not nullify the grace of God," but Phillips may best express it with, "I refuse to make nonsense of the grace of God," or perhaps the Jerusalem Bible, "I cannot bring myself to give up God's gift."

This shows that it is quite possible for Christians to leave unopened God's precious gift of grace, which is to lay it aside unclaimed, or to make nonsense of it. Being the pragmatic individualists that we are, a "do-it-yourself" people, we can't believe there are really any free lunches, not even in religion. Grace can't really be a completely free gift, we figure, for we have to do our part — by repenting or being baptized, or going to church, or something! — for it is illogical that God would freely bestow his grace apart from our cooperation. It is our pragmatism, our humanism, our fleshly pride — yes, our logic — that causes us to do what Paul sought to avoid, nullify the gift by failing to realize that it is free, *unconditionally* free. Of course it is illogical, that is what makes it grace. There is no logic in giving heaven itself to people that do not deserve it.

This is why we've never been able to accept the astounding truth set forth in Rom. 5:15 where Paul contrasts the penalty given to those who shared in Adam's fall (death) and those who benefitted from the grace of God in Christ (life). Notice how Phillips has it: "Nor is the effect of God's gift the same as the effect of that one man's sin. For in the one case one man's sin brought its inevitable judgment, and the result was condemnation. But, in the other, countless men's sins are met with the free gift of grace, and the result is justification before God."

The best explanation of this is what Paul says in 1 Cor. 15:22: "For as in Adam all die, so also in Christ shall all be made alive." If we are blind to this staggering truth it is because we can't see grace for what it is. The apostle is saying, clear and simple, that in Adam all mankind died — *all* he says — and in Christ all mankind is made alive or given life — again, *all* humanity is given life in Christ. If the first *all* means everyone the second *all* means everyone. That is grace!

This means that in Adam's fall all people died, but when Christ died on the cross he died for all people and saved all people. Everybody is saved! That is the beauty of the gospel and that is why it is good news. To tell everyone that he or she is lost is bad news. Our message should be that God has saved you through Christ! Won't you accept it? Only those who persistently and finally reject the free gift offered will be lost. The Bible again and again makes it clear who will be lost, those who *reject* the gospel, thus refusing the free gift. Everyone else will be saved.

President Nixon's pardon illustrates this. He was guilty before the law. He did not deserve the pardon. There was nothing he did or could do that merited it. He was utterly helpless. A representative of President Ford delivered the pardon. Nixon only needed to accept the free gift by signing a document of acceptance. He said it was the most difficult thing he ever did.

Why was it so difficult? For the same reason grace as a free gift is always difficult for the pride of man to accept. If Nixon had been told he deserved the pardon for his devoted service to his country, it would not have been difficult for him to accept. Neither would it have been grace. Nixon's pardon was an unconditional free gift of grace, no strings attached. Only the enjoyment of the grace was conditional. He had to accept it

An illustration I borrow from Alexander Campbell may be better. Campbell wanted to show that God's grace is unconditionally bestowed to all mankind, apart from any worth, merit, or works on man's part. But the appropriation and enjoyment of the grace is conditional. To illustrate this he told a story of a ship at sea in peril in a raging storm. It was sinking and all on board were lost An old captain of the sea saw their predicament from the shore, and out of the goodness and mercy of his heart sent his son in a lifeboat into the dangerous sea to the doomed ship. The son cried to them amidst the storm that they were saved, beckoning them into the lifeboat. That is grace, Campbell said, sheer grace, apart from any initiative on the part of the lost. The bestowal and presence of the grace was unconditional.

But, Campbell goes on, to appropriate the free gift of grace and to enjoy its benefits, the men on the doomed ship had to get in the lifeboat. Like Peter did on Pentecost in Acts 2, the son could have cried out to the men on the doomed ship, "Save yourselves," but this can only mean something like "Accept the gift" or "Take advantage of what my father has done for you." It would be nonsense to say that the men did anything to merit the grace. They merely reached out and accepted an unconditional free gift of grace. That of course they had to do, but that made the grace no less free.

That is where baptism comes in. It is God's way of having us accept the gift. And even baptism is not something we do as much as it is something done to us. Baptism is an act of grace, appropriating for us the free gift.

And even if the men did, once in the lifeboat, cooperate with the son in maneuvering the boat through the tempestuous sea to shore, all of them rowing for their lives, their salvation was still only by the grace of the father. They "worked out their salvation with fear and trembling" because they had already been saved by grace, not in order to be saved by their own works. That is why we do good works, not to be saved but because we are saved.

While no illustration is perfect, that one goes far in showing what grace is and how we are to respond to it. Donald Barnhouse is credited with saying that love that goes upward is worship, love that goes outward is affection, and love that stoops is grace. That says it. Grace always stoops, to the point of being extravagant. Why should God give his Son to die for a recreant bunch like us? We are saved only because the great God of heaven chose to stoop to our level and lift us up.

The Church of Christ must boldly claim such great texts on grace as Eph. 2:8-9 as its own: "By grace you have been saved through faith, and that not of yourselves; it is the gift of God, not of works, lest anyone should boast." And Paul's great conclusion must be our own: "Therefore we conclude that a man is justified by faith apart from the deeds of the law" (Rom. 3:28). And we must plug into some of Paul's not's — "Not having my own righteousness, which is from the law" (Philip. 3:9), and "Not by works of righteousness which we have done" (Tit. 3:5). Let's claim the free gift and make it our own. It is by God's grace, not by our works. It is mercy that makes us righteous, not our own goodness. It is by nothing that we do ourselves.

Only grace will free us from our legalism. Only grace will deliver us from the backwater of our sectarianism. Only grace will give us the assurance of our salvation. So long as we are deceived into believing that "we have to do it" and that righteousness is at least partly our own doing, we can never be sure of our standing with God. We must realize that God's grace is not auctioned off to the highest bidder. We can do nothing to merit it, we cannot work enough to earn it, we cannot be good enough to deserve it, we cannot be rich enough to buy it, we cannot muster enough power to wrest it. Grace is God's free gift, all because he loves us, abundantly and extravagantly.

When we "stand" in the grace of God, trusting in his goodness and mercy, then love, joy, and peace will flood our hearts. We will then be a more gracious people, magnanimous, full of life and enthusiasm, eager to praise God for his great mercy. We will take ourselves less seriously and be able to laugh at our foibles. We will not be so uptight, we'll quit worrying, be less critical of others, more accepting, more forgiving.

It is the grace of God that has made the Church of Christ a great people, but that grace is waiting to do much more with us. If we will resolve now to be a grace-empowered people, not laying aside the free gift, not nullifying it, we will be destined for spiritual heights that "you would not believe if told" (Hab. 1:5).

The grace is there, stooped at our feet. Let's bend down and plug in and get going!

Chapter 15:
Discover the Good in the
Good News

There is a story about the disenchanted member of the Church of Christ who confronted every preacher who came to his congregation for the annual "Gospel Meeting" with the question, "What is good about the good news?" They would all say that the gospel means good news, but he wasn't hearing anything good in the gospel that they preached. It was rather bad news, or so it seemed to him. When he failed year after year to get a satisfactory answer to his question, he concluded that he was not going to hear good news at the Church of Christ and left us.

The story may be apocryphal or it may be overstated, but for those of us who know the Churches of Christ there is a disturbing familiarity to it. It is a question we must come to terms with, *Where is the good news in the gospel that we preach?*

It would be deemed both presumptuous and irresponsible to say that after all these years the Churches of Christ do not even know what the gospel is, and that they preach more bad news than good news. We do of course preach what we understand to be the gospel, but the question the man asked in the story prevails — Where is the good news in the gospel that we preach?

A look at some of the fallacies we commit in reference to the gospel will serve to put the question in perspective. We have been critical of big-time evangelists like Billy Graham for "not preaching the gospel" since he does not preach baptism. We fail to apply this same rule to the apostle Paul who insisted that "Christ sent me not to baptize but to preach the gospel." If this means anything it means that there is a distinction between preaching the gospel and preaching baptism. Did any New Testament evangelist ever "preach" baptism? They preached "the gospel of the grace of

God" and they preached" Jesus Christ and him crucified," but did they ever proclaim any ordinance? Was it not always a person, the Person of Jesus Christ, that they proclaimed?

Would it not follow then that anyone who proclaims Jesus as the risen Christ and the Savior of the world is preaching the good news of the gospel, *all* of the gospel? Granted, the likes of Billy Graham may err in not properly instructing people how to respond to the good news by repenting of their sins and being baptized for the remission of their sins like Peter did on the day of Pentecost. But if one preaches Jesus Christ as the Savior of the world he is preaching the gospel, apart from what he might or might not say about baptism.

Did not Peter preach the gospel, all of the gospel, before he had reason to say anything about baptism? Acts 2:37 says, "When they heard this, they were cut to the heart . . ." What was the *this?* Was it not the facts that make up the good news, such as "This Jesus God raised up, of which we are all witnesses?" It was the gospel that cut them to the heart. The record says they asked, "Men and brethren, what shall we do?" It is only at this point that Peter says anything about baptism. Suppose the response had been negative and they had turned away without making any inquiry about what they should do? In that case Peter would have said nothing about baptism, for it was an act of response to the gospel, not the gospel itself.

Peter told what was good about the good news before he was asked about baptism. That is in fact why they were cut to the heart, the power of the good news. Preaching baptism doesn't cut people to the heart, though it might convert them to an ordinance. And sometimes even the good news does not convict people. In other places in Acts, as in chap. 4, the apostles preach the gospel, but there is no response like that on Pentecost, and so nothing is said about baptism. But they no less preached the gospel.

Would it have been any different if in the history of Church of Christ preaching we had concentrated on proclaiming Jesus Christ as the good news of our salvation and said nothing about baptism except as people made inquiry as they did on Pentecost? Haven't we been guilty of preaching an ordinance more than a Person? It is understandable that a hungry soul such as the one in our story would badger our preachers about where the good news was in the gospel they preached.

Recent studies by some of our own scholars reveal that there has not been much good news in what we have called "gospel preaching." In a 1988 article in the *Gospel Advocate*, F. W. Mattox explains that Church of Christ preachers have left it to "denominational preachers" to preach grace, faith, and the atonement while they "went about straightening out their misunderstanding of the place, action, and order of faith, repentance, and baptism in obtaining church membership." Mattox notes that while others preached the atonement of Christ but not baptism, we preached baptism but not the atonement of Christ. Others preached Christ while we "straightened out" those who so preached. Alas for the iron bed of Procrustes!

Back in 1937 K. C. Moser wrote a tract on "Are We Preaching The Gospel?" [4] in which he charged that the Churches of Christ were not preaching the gospel. By the gospel he meant the good news of Jesus Christ and him crucified. For much of his life Moser charged that we are not a Cross-centered, grace-oriented people, and even when we "preach" baptism it is treated as an arbitrary command unrelated to the Cross. In a reference to one of Harry Emerson Fosdick's books, in which he finds not even a hint of Christ dying for our sins, Moser issued a stunning indictment of Church of Christ preaching: "If Mr. Fosdick has REJECTED the gospel, others have NEGLECTED it." Moser examined a book of 50 Church of Christ sermons and found in none of them more than a passing reference to the gospel.

Bill Love, former minister to the Bering Drive Church of Christ in Houston, in a book titled *The Core Gospel* has studied the content of preaching in the Restoration Movement during its first four generations, from the early 1800's to the 1950's. His aim was to determine to what extent Restoration preachers preached the core gospel (the Cross) in comparison to New Testament preachers. His findings are disturbing, for while the NT preachers referred to the Cross in all the 33 sermons in the NT (100% of the time), Restoration preachers in the hundreds of sermons that Bill studied referred to the Cross only 25% of the time.

Love's study reveals that there was a continual decline in the preaching of the Cross from the generation of Stone and Campbell (56% of their sermons pointed to the Cross) to the generation of G. C. Brewer and Foy Wallace (23% of the time). In the first two generations, before the Church of Christ was a separate church, preachers referred to the cross an average of 52% of the time, while in the two generations of Church of Christ history our preachers averaged only 25%.

I could not help but notice that the most irenic and unity-minded of our preachers were Cross-centered (Barton Stone, who never had a debate, pointed to the Cross 82 % of the time), while the more controversial did not (J. D. Tant referred to the Cross only 12% of the time). I was pleased to see that Hardeman and Wallace scored as high in Bill's study as they did, 41% and 42% respectively. But the over-all findings are alarming. Part of Bill's conclusion is: "Our focus moved from Christ crucified to his church, a subtle but destructive shift," and then adds "Once our sickness took hold, we grew weaker and weaker, more and more anemic. Without the gospel we lost touch with the source of our faith."

The Church of Christ is sick and without the gospel? If this charge is anything like a true appraisal, it is clear enough what we must do to be saved. We must discover the good in the good news. What is good about the good news is that God's mercy is as magnanimous and as far reaching as the universe itself. God's love has no limits and his grace is unconditional. We must discover, as an astronomer sights a "new" constellation in the heavens, the magnificent grace and mercy passages in Scripture and saturate our preaching with them.

Here are a few of the great truths about the good news that the Churches of Christ have virtually ignored. If we would begin to emphasize these passages in our teaching and preaching as we have passages about baptism and the church, it is predictable that a great change would be wrought among us.

"For God sent the Son into the world, not to condemn the world, but that the world might be saved through him" (Jn. 3:17).

"And I, when I am lifted up from the earth, will draw all men to myself" (Jn. 12:32).

"For I did not come to judge the world but to save the world" (Jn. 12:47).

"So that by the grace of God he might taste of death for every one" (Heb. 2:9).

"For the grace of God has appeared for the salvation of all men" (Tit. 2:11).

"For as in Adam all die, so also in Christ shall all be made alive" (1 Cor. 15:22).

"And he is the expiation for our sins, and not for ours only but also for the sins of the whole world" (1 Jn. 2:2).

"For the love of God controls us, because we are convinced that one has died for all; therefore all have died. And he died for all, that those who live might live no longer for themselves but for him who for their sake died and was raised" (2 Cor. 5:14-15).

"In Christ God was reconciling the world to himself, not counting their trespasses against them, and entrusting to us the ministry of reconciliation" (2 Cor. 5:19).

These passages all have something precious in common: each one tells us that Christ died for the sins of the entire world, all humankind, every single person, absolutely and unconditionally. However sinful your life has been, Christ died for you. You are saved by his grace, which is God's free gift. Now that is good news! We are not preaching good news when we tell people they are lost and bound for doom and destruction. They are saved and bound for heaven! That is what is good about the good news.

So, there are two "gospels" we can preach. We can tell the world it is lost and must repent to be saved. Or we can tell the world what the Bible says in the passages quoted, that just as in Adam all died so in Christ are all made alive, that all people are saved, so one only needs to accept the free gift. We can look at the world and say every one is lost except those that the Bible says will be saved, or we can look at the world and say every one is saved except those that the Bible says will be lost. Which is good news: You are lost, therefore repent; or You are saved, won't you accept it?

Jesus is the Savior of the world, not the *potential* Savior. He has not died for all men *if* . . . He has died for all men (period!) Christ died for you; you are saved by his grace, no strings attached. Only accept it. That is the good news of the gospel. Everyone is saved! The only exceptions are those the Bible clearly states will be lost — those who persistently and finally refuse to accept the free gift. The Bible condemns only those who refuse and continue to refuse to believe and obey Christ.

So, the Church of Christ has had it backwards and has consequently preached bad news. We have preached that everyone is lost, while the Bible teaches that everyone is saved. Everyone is saved except those who refuse the free gift. The Bible tells us who will be lost, those who "refuse to acknowledge God" (Rom. 1:28) even after he unconditionally bestowed his grace upon them. Everyone else is saved.

That's the answer to the disheartened member of the Church of Christ who wanted to know what is good about the good news. What an answer we have for such ones. What is good about the good news is that Jesus Christ has saved the whole world, every single soul, by dying on the Cross for us, freely and unconditionally. Wow, that is good news!

Let's preach the glorious good news. God has saved you through Christ, taking away all your sins, as the above verses teach. Won't you accept it through faith and baptism? Only those who refuse will be lost. Or to put it another way, everyone is of "the elect" (another subject we virtually ignore) except those who persistently refuse to believe and obey.

Chapter 16:
Recover the Dynamic of Spirit-filled Gatherings in Homes

Let's face it, the Churches of Christ are in the doldrums. Our services are often boring, lifeless, gloomy. I'm convinced that our most loyal members attend regularly because they are just that, loyal, and not because they find it joyous and exciting. We are not growing. An outsider would never see us as imaginative, creative, or innovative. Except for some encouraging exceptions, we are not a changing people and we are not out on the cutting edge. We are going to have to get with it or we will not be saved.

That other mainline denominations are in the same predicament does not justify our own stagnation. As a well-known automobile executive says on TV: *Lead the way, follow, or get out of the way.* It is not all that different with the churches. If we don't get with it, we will not have to worry about what will happen to us. We'll be left behind.

At the heart of our problem, as well as other churches, is that we are caught in the trappings of our own institutionalism — or *churchism* might be the word. We have expensive edifices to pay for and to maintain, staffs to support, programs to fund. Our Achilles heel is the System. The System resists change, except occasional cosmetic change. Nothing real or substantial. The System demands conformity, and it is uneasy with thinking people around, especially a thinking preacher or a preacher that says something.

The System must maintain the status quo, and it must preserve itself at all cost. This is why it seeks to keep everyone satisfied by reacting rather than acting. And most significantly, the System is tied to the building. Regular church attendance, along with generous giving, is the essence of "faithfulness."

This brings me to the one thing above most everything else that we must do to be saved. We must recover — or is it *discover?* — the great lost secret of primitive Christianity. That secret was the dynamic of joyous, Spirit-filled gatherings in homes. Primitive Christianity knew nothing of buildings that never seem to get paid for. They did not have to bother with building an educational wing or getting the parking lot resurfaced, which are major tasks for the modern church. The early churches were house churches; as they grew they took in more homes. It wasn't until the third or fourth centuries that they had edifices and eventually "sanctuaries." This is the great secret of the early church that we are indifferent to — they were house churches while we are cathedral churches. They had a Holy Spirit-complex while we have an edifice-complex.

The edifice-complex has pews lined up one behind the other where we look behind each other's ears and may not even know the people who sit on the same pew — and may not even speak to them, week after week. The Holy Spirit-complex expressed itself in the home with sisters and brothers gathered in a circle, sharing their stories from out there in the world, drinking and eating together, rejoicing together. They were usually a persecuted people who took refuge in each other in the family circle, which was truly the Body of Christ.

Acts 2:46 tells us about them: "And day by day, attending the temple together and breaking bread in their homes, they partook of food with glad and generous hearts." There are four references to "the church in thy house" and at least 20 instances in Acts and the letters where Christians met in homes. They were in the temple grounds, in synagogues, in the streets, in homes, but they never "went to church" in a building set apart for that purpose, not for at least 200 years. This does not mean that it is wrong for us to have buildings, but we need to realize what we have allowed the System to do to us.

In home gatherings they knew each other and grew close to one another. Everyone could take part. They didn't have to worry about a

woman "getting in the pulpit" since there was
no pulpit. They shared together, with each part
functioning unto the edifying of the Body.
They did not look to an employed functionary
to deliver sermons; there were no sermons.
They didn't have to worry about how to dress;
if one came in smelling of fish it was OK. If a
congregation needed to expand, it took in
another home; if it needed to be dissolved, no
problem since it had no mortgage to pay off. In
the home they were "members one of another,"
rejoicing in the Spirit. The great lost secret of
the primitive church is that they were
empowered with the Holy Spirit in home
gatherings.

I do not conclude from all this that we
should close down our buildings. We cannot
be the first century church, but as the 21st
century church we can discover the great lost
secret of the primitive church and make it
applicable to our own time. Our buildings can
be used for small group gatherings as well as
large congregational meetings, but they should
be more intimate and open to the leading of the
Spirit than the usual Sunday school

arrangement. Let eight to ten men and women gather in a circle each Sunday and Wednesday evenings long enough to get intimately acquainted. They could start by sharing what Jesus means to them, and from there they could talk about their fears, hopes, problems, family, etc. They would learn to pray together as a family of sisters and brothers, and they would eventually unburden their souls to each other.

Along with this we could get away from our buildings and into homes more than we now do. A congregation could take a Sunday evening each month to meet in homes, with something like ten to twelve people to each home. We need to be in each other's home, come to know each other better, love each other more, learn to pray and share together in a way that cannot be done in the big "sanctuary" at church. In such an atmosphere the Holy Spirit can teach us more about the meaning of unity and fellowship.

The same circle could continue meeting on a long term basis, but in time the circles could rotate so that a greater number in the church would know each other more personally. It is when we can share our long-kept secrets with each other, along with our hang-ups, that we really become "members one of another" where when one suffers all suffer and when one rejoices all rejoice. This is Body life and this is the great lost secret of the primitive church.

These small groups are also ideal for friendship evangelism. Outsiders can often be introduced to spiritual things in the informal atmosphere of a private home rather than in a church setting. The joy and spontaneity of the home gatherings can also transfer to some degree to the public assemblies if only we will be less rigid. When our services are revved up and there is "a sweet spirit that fills this place" we will be more inclined to share it with others. Who wants to invite a friend to a boring service?

To discover the lost secret we must be more open to change. We must get beyond the institutional church to Christ himself. We must become vulnerable to each other as sisters and brothers, fervent in the Spirit, serving the Lord.

To do this we do not need to think *big* in the sense of huge congregations and mega-churches. The lost secret is not big programs, large crowds or huge budgets, just as it is not necessarily big government and big business that makes a nation truly great. We may rightfully become disillusioned with "big" things. Our hopes might better lie with quiet processes and small circles where transforming events may take place.

Chapter 17:
Heed the Principles Set Forth by Barton W. Stone

It would be understandable if concerned Americans appealed to the virtues of Benjamin Franklin, Thomas Jefferson, or Abraham Lincoln as a possible answer to the predicament this nation faces in the 1990's. In times of crisis we look to our past for possible clues on what we might do to solve our problems. Those who have gone before and who struggled with similar problems often have wisdom to bequeath. But we are slow to learn the lesson of history. Lincoln, for instance, warned that a nation cannot endure half free and half slave. Yet we continue to be enslaved in part by racism, injustice, and poverty.

In the same way the Church of Christ might save itself from obscurantism, obsolescence, and irrelevance (as well as exclusivism, sectarianism, and isolationism) by an appeal to a nobler era of its history. Warnings that we are in trouble are being heard from unexpected places. In listening to some of the tapes of the recent lectureship at Pepperdine, I heard one speaker, who was frequently interrupted by applause by his large audience, cry out in no uncertain terms, "The Church of Christ is dead!" He was calling for change, particularly in reference to the ministry of women, "bringing the women into the church," as he put it.

Those who are calling for change these days are not always aware of the contributions that can be made by our forebears. They too went through the crucible of change, and out of their struggle comes wisdom that would serve us well. The lessons from our past are there for us to learn. Must we go on making the same mistakes over and over again.

As an illustration of what I mean I refer to but one document, a single letter in fact, by Barton W. Stone, entitled most appropriately for our purposes, "An Address to the Churches of Christ." It was written in 1832 and grows out of the drama and trauma of the union between the Stone and Campbell churches that had taken place in Lexington, Kentucky, that same year. In this address Stone was seeking to effect the union further by addressing problems that troubled the Movement both then and now.

So, in this installment I am saying that the Church of Christ can be saved by taking heed to the principles set forth by Barton Stone in his address to Churches of Christ 160 years ago. That he was not wholly ignored back then is one reason why the Movement enjoyed substantial success and remained united for at least two generations. It would be well if this address were published in its entirety as a resource for change in our time. It is in order for us to consider the main ideas set forth.

In addressing "the Churches of Christ," Stone is using but one of three names our people used in the early years of our history, the others being Christian Churches and Disciples of Christ, the latter being preferred by Alexander Campbell. But generally our people used all three names and they applied to but one people, one church. It is a travesty that the Movement eventually divided so thoroughly that we now have three branches (a euphemism for factions?), each known by one of these names, mainly.

It is incredible how well Stone read the future as well as the present in what he said to the Churches of Christ in 1832. Early on in the Address he warned against unwritten creeds, which he considered more dangerous than written ones. The purpose of both, he noted, "is to exclude from fellowship the man who dissents from them." He observes that there are those who clamor against (written) creeds and yet have creeds (unwritten) of their own, and they are as intolerant toward those who dissent from their creeds as those who make written creeds are toward their dissenters.

Stone could have added that it is always the "liberal" or the innovator that motivates creed-making, for creeds are calculated to defend orthodoxy. Creeds are designed to draw lines and to defend the party line. Stone was right in preferring written creeds to unwritten ones, for written ones are more reliable and predictable. In unwritten creeds people make up their rules as they go along, tailoring the creed to fit the occasion or the one "to be marked."

What pain we would have avoided had the wisdom of this pioneer reached our ears. With ne'er a (written) creed in sight we have been creed-makers, and, like Stone said, we have used them to draw lines on each other and to exclude one another from fellowship. We have made creeds of our opinions, whether in reference to theories like millennialism, questions such as marriage and divorce, or methods like instrumental music or Sunday schools. It is of course appropriate for each of us to follow his own conviction in reference to any of these, but it is not all right to make a creed out of them. Creed-making makes parties, whether they be written or unwritten creeds, and that is what lies behind all our divisions.

Barton W. Stone probably said more about the Holy Spirit's ministry in the life of the Christian than any of our leading pioneers. In this Address he refers to the gift of the Holy Spirit as "more necessary" than faith, reformation, and immersion. The Holy Spirit more important than baptism? In an open letter to Churches of Christ? Most of us would not have supposed that we have that kind of emphasis in our early history. Stone names the gift of the Holy Spirit as "the crowning blessing of all blessings." He quotes Gal. 3:14 and Acts 5:32 to show that the Spirit is received through faith and that it is given to those that obey Christ.

In this connection Stone laid out the plan of salvation in a way that somehow got lost before today's Church of Christ came along: "God's plan appears to be this, that whoever believes, repents and is baptized, or obeys the gospel, shall be saved, shall receive remission of sins, and the gift of the Holy Spirit."

Stone was always emphatic about the Holy Spirit. One of his favorite sermons was "Four

Kinds of Unity," three of which he named as false unities. Head union, book union, water union are not true union, while fire unity, the radiating Spirit of God within us, is what makes us really one. In another context he named the difference between the Holy Spirit and the sectarian spirit. The Holy Spirit, he said, bears the fruit of humility, forbearance, love, peace, and unity. The sectarian spirit leads to pride, preeminence, intolerance, and opposition to those of another party. He went on to say that it is the sectarian spirit that causes discord, strife, and division. *(Christian Messenger,* 1832, p. 21).

In the light of such teaching it would hardly be appropriate to label the modern Churches of Christ as Stoneites. Somewhere along the line we forgot that the Holy Spirit had ever been given, or we supposed he went into retirement in some past age. And how many of us would say that the Holy Spirit is more important than baptism?

While in this Address Stone makes a strong case for immersion, he stops short of saying that only the immersed are Christians. He put it this way: "We have no doubt that multitudes have been changed, are pious, and will ultimately be saved with an everlasting salvation who have not been immersed." He went on to concede that immersion is God's plan, but that we cannot hold God to his plan and not allow him to pardon a humble penitent without immersion. He added, "Far from us be this sentiment."

But this sentiment, a hard-line, legalistic position on immersion for remission of sins, has not been far from us in the Church of Christ. We can see that it did not begin with Stone.

Stone was hopeful that this Address would help to unite the Stone and Campbell movements despite their differences. He therefore emphasized what he considered a crucial principle of their plea for unity: *Christians may differ without dividing.* He referred to two differences between their churches at this time, which troubled people on both sides. The Campbell people placed greater emphasis upon immersion for remission of sins than the Stone churches, and the Campbell churches broke bread every first day while the Stone people didn't.

This diversity of doctrine and practice led Stone to emphasize what had characterized the Movement from the outset: "We who profess to stand upon the Bible alone, and contend that opinions of truth should not be made terms of fellowship — shall we be intolerant towards each other because we may differ in our opinions? Forbid it, Heaven!"

Here Stone is telling us what we must do to be saved. We must cease and desist from making our own interpretation of what we believe to be the truth (an opinion, Stone calls it) a test of fellowship. And he says this includes such matters as the design of baptism and the frequency of the Lord's supper. Hear him: "All believe that immersion is baptism," referring to the Stone and Campbell people, "why should they who submit to the one baptism contend and separate because they do not exactly view every design of it alike?"

Stone went on to say what should be proclaimed in every Church of Christ in the land today: "If you think your brother in error, labor in the spirit of love and meekness to convince him; but imposing zeal against him will only harden him against any good impression you would make. It will probably stir up strife and ultimately destroy love, the bond of union."

Note the words "imposing zeal against him," such as in a big debate. It was not by accident that Barton Stone never had a debate, which is seldom "in the spirit of love and meekness" that he called for in his Address. Here we have the recipe for our salvation from "Father Stone" as they called him in his old age. We have fought, debated, and divided ourselves to the point that love, the bond of union, has been destroyed.

We must repent of our ugly, sectarian past and resolve to follow Stone's advice when he went on to say in his Address to us, the Churches of Christ: "A little longer forbearance with each others' weakness, and truth will triumph."

In that Address the old reformer went out to give expression to his motto, which is today engraved in stone under his name on the cenotaph that stands in front of the Disciples of Christ Historical Society in Nashville: "Let the unity of Christians be our polar star." The motto was inspired by Jesus' prayer for unity in John 17. We are to be ONE so that the world might be WON, our Lord says in that prayer.

With our eyes cast on that polar star, the unity of all believers, and our hearts and minds resolved to do our part to answer the Lord's prayer so that the world may believe, we can get back on track and save ourselves as well as others.

Chapter 18:
Bring Women into the Church

In the ninth installment of this series I stated that if the Church of Christ is to be saved it must cease to be male-dominated. I gave a list of steps we could take immediately to include women in the ministry of the church, public and private alike, all without violating either our conscience or the Scriptures. If you have not read that piece, I urge you to do so, for I believe you will find it liberating.

In this installment I want to say more about the ministry of women, and in doing so I will urge that we "bring the women into the church," as a speaker put it recently at the Pepperdine University lectureship. I am persuaded that he said it as it is, as startling as it sounds, for we have virtually left women out of the church. They are members, of course, and their presence has always been crucial, but they are left out of the corporate worship of the church.

So, in this installment I will ride coattail on the Pepperdine lecturer and say if the Church of Christ is to be saved it must bring women into the church. That means *really* bring them to the forefront of the work of the church and cease and desist with our present male-dominated services. I'll speak plainly, as did our brother at Pepperdine: *We leave our women out, and that is a sin!*

The Pepperdine lecturer also said, "The Church of Christ is dead!" Perhaps he meant we are dying, but whatever he meant he related it to the way we have been treating our sisters in Christ. To be revived, he was saying, we must come to terms with the one line in Scripture that must be the arbiter for this entire question: *There is neither male nor female, for you are all one in Christ Jesus* (Gal. 3:28).

If that passage means anything it means that gender is not to be made a test of fellowship or ministry, such as, "She can't do that because she is a woman." Paul himself may have sometimes fallen short of that ideal of perfect equality, due to the pressures of custom, as in the case of slavery, which he tolerated, and which is forbidden in that same passage, "There is neither bond nor free." If socio-economic conditions had been different, Paul might not have said what he did about women and slaves, tolerating their unequal treatment.

To put it another way, Paul almost certainly would not say to the 21st century church what he said to the first century church about women and slaves (and Jews!). But still he laid down the principle that applies to all generations because it so reflects the mind of Christ: In the Church of Christ there is to be no distinction between slaves and freedmen, Jews and Gentiles, men and women! We have to recognize that this was the ideal that even he was not always able to effect due to the conditions beyond his control.

Take, for example, this absolute rule to the church at Corinth: "It is shameful for women to speak in church" (1 Cor. 14:35). He allows for no exception, not in that context anyway. To whom is it shameful for a woman to speak in church. To God? To Paul? To the church? It probably refers to none of these, but to the general public, and this due to biases associated with temple prostitution in Corinth. It was shameful for a woman to be aggressive and assertive, domineering over men, as they did in the temple of Diana in Ephesus, to which city he also wrote about this.

Are we to take a rule like this and apply it to the whole church for all time to come? Is it a shame for a woman to speak in a church in Paris or London or New York in 2010? We live in a culture where women speak in parliament, in the halls of congress, in corporate board rooms, in the public media — with no shame attached to it at all. A shame for a woman to speak in church? It may have been in the context of the problem Paul was dealing with, but not now.

The biblical grounds for leaving women out of the church is due to a faulty hermeneutics, namely, an indiscriminate application of Scripture, or supposing that if a passage applies to a given situation it applies to all situations for all time to come.

There is hardly any question but what the Bible lays down certain limitations on the ministry of women, such as in 1 Tim. 2:11-12: "Let a woman learn in silence with all submission. And I do not permit a woman to teach or to have authority over a man, but to be in silence." As we shall see, the apostle had what he believed were good reasons for such a restriction, and we may assume that Timothy, the evangelist to whom he was writing, took such instructions seriously as he ministered in Ephesus.

It is unfaithful to Scripture to find artful ways to "explain away" such passages. The apostle did not want women speaking (or praying) in the churches like men did (period). It is true that he creates a problem when elsewhere he calls for women to both "pray and prophesy," albeit with her head covered, as in 1 Cor. 11:5. It is generally conceded that prophesying means teaching. Is she to be silent as in the first text or is she to pray and prophesy as in the second?

I am not sure these passages can be reconciled. One might say, I suppose, that to Paul a woman is to be silent in church, ordinarily; if and when she prays and prophesies, as per her special gift, she is to do so only with her head covered. The covered head would allay the criticism that called for the restriction to start with: assertive women are associated with all the shenanigans going on in temple prostitute worship.

The reasons Paul gives for his restriction in 1 Timothy may appear odd to the modern church. "For Adam was formed first, then Eve," was Paul's first reason for women being silent. I would have difficulty telling a young sister who is majoring in music at the university that she cannot sing in church because of Adam's priority in creation. Paul's second reason is hardly more persuasive. Are you likely to explain to a sister who lectures in sociology in college that she is forbidden to teach a man in church because of Eve's priority in transgression?

If those reasons were important to Paul, one is left to wonder why he would ever allow a woman to pray and prophesy even with her head covered. Paul must have learned such reasoning in his rabbinical education. The rabbis were all men, you know. It was in fact unlawful for a woman to even study the law! The reasons Paul gave for a woman's submission may well have been persuasive to his readers. But today? Don't centuries make a difference with some Scripture, while other passages are so crucial as to transcend all time and all cultures, as does: "There is neither Jew nor Greek, there is neither slave nor free, there is neither male nor female; for you are all one in Christ Jesus" (Gal. 3:28)

Whether Paul was consistent or not, we must grant that he imposed restrictions upon women in contexts where this seemed appropriate to him. But it is reasonable for us to conclude that this was a temporary measure growing out of the Jewish! Greek culture of the times, and is not a rule for the church universal for all generations to come. Paul, of course, did not think of his instructions as "temporary," but for all churches for all time to come, but he had no way of knowing how things would be in cultures not yet born. To impose silence on women in today's church and say she can't teach a man appears to most Christians as a violation of "the sense of Scripture" and the one sure rule of interpretation, "the spirit of Christ."

It is hardly conceivable that Jesus Christ would say to his community today: "The women must be silent; I forbid them to teach." Paul had his reasons for saying that in his situation, and we are to accept that; but he also ruled that the woman was not to have "braided (or plaited) hair or gold or pearls or costly clothing" (1 Tim. 2:9). Does this mean the same thing today?

We have no problem in saying "Does not apply" to a lot of things in the New Testament, some of which are stated as commands, such as foot washing (both a command and an example) and the holy kiss (commanded four times). And from these same passages in Paul we have the likes of head coverings and long hair, as well as the injunction against braided hair. In Acts 15 we have the apostles gathered with the whole church, and with the guidance of the Holy Spirit they laid down four "necessary things" — *necessary* it reads in verse 28. We have no problem at all in totally ignoring three of the four. (It is debatable how seriously we take the fourth one, which enjoins against fornication!) Why? Custom, we say. What is so wrong about applying the same logic to these passages about the subjugation of women?

We only need to realize the place of women in those days to understand why there would be such restrictions. While the place of woman in the home was honored in Jewish culture, her position as a whole was degrading. In Jewish law she was a thing rather than a person. To teach a woman was casting pearls to swine. In their prayers the men thanked God that they were not born a Gentile, a slave, or a woman. Men would not speak to a woman in public, not even their own wife or daughter. When walking in public the woman would walk behind the man. She had no part in the synagogue service; she often sat in the gallery where she could not be seen. Scriptures were read in the synagogue, but never by a woman. She could not even teach a school.

Paul's restriction on women in 1 Timothy, along with a similar restriction in 1 Cor. 14:34-35, where it is added that if they want to learn they are to ask their husbands at home, was also influenced by Greek culture where the place of the woman was also debased. The Greek woman led a confined life, living in her own quarters and not even appearing at meals. She never appeared in the street alone. The aggressive women were associated with the prostitute cults at the Temple of Aphrodite in Corinth and the Temple of Diana in Ephesus, the two cities where Paul had imposed his restrictions. If the women in a church in a Greek city had assumed an active role, the church would have been thought of as a haven of loose women. This is why the veiled head, suggesting submission, would have blunted this charge.

Considering this background, it is impressive that women in these earliest churches had as much freedom in ministry as they had. Early Christianity went far in liberating women. The church began on Pentecost with the prophetic cry that "Your sons and your daughters shall prophesy" (Acts 2:17). It was a woman who was chosen to bear and nourish the Christ child, and women served with him in heralding the good news of the kingdom. It was four women among his disciples that were there when he was crucified.

Women were ministers in the earliest congregations. Phoebe was a deacon (Rom. 16:1); Euodia and Syntyche labored in the gospel with Paul (Philip. 4:2-3); several were prophets (Acts 21:9); older women taught the younger (Tit. 2:3); it was women that helped to prepare Timothy for his work as an evangelist (2 Tim. 1:5); Priscilla taught a man the way of the Lord more perfectly (Acts 18:26).

So, when it comes to "those passages against women teachers" we should at least recognize that there are two sides to the question. I don't see that they have to be reconciled, for our task in the 21st century is not to do precisely as they did, but to do for our generation what they did for theirs, bring in the kingdom of God. And our men and women should be at it today just as their men and women were at it back then, but not necessarily in exactly the same way.

In reading Paul we are to understand that he sometimes speaks for the Lord and sometimes for himself. He draws such distinctions as "I command, yet not I but the Lord" (1 Cor. 7:10), and "I, not the Lord, say" (1 Cor. 7:10). We cannot always be sure when it is Paul and when it is the Lord. There is a difference, isn't there, whatever we make of apostolic authority? Most of us are inclined to pay greater heed to the words printed in red. What our Lord says is absolute and for all time and for all ages. Some of Paul's injunctions may be more temporary and circumstantial, though still to be taken seriously since he was an apostle of Christ. But not absolute.

One might disagree with Paul, both in what he sometimes did and what he sometimes said. He is a problem to us when he "kept the law" by shaving his head and undergoing temple purification (Acts 21:26). And he probably said more than he should have said in Gal. 5:12 when he scored the Judaizers who wanted to circumcise everybody, a passage most versions tone down. When you read it in the Jerusalem Bible, Paul wishes his enemies would circumcise themselves, and adds, "I would like to see the knife slip."

An important passage in Paul is where he says "Follow me as I follow Christ." I'll buy that. But does he always follow Christ?

You will observe that Paul enjoins women's submission with: "I do not permit a woman to teach, etc." Is that the same as Christ saying it? Is even Paul saying it for all time and for all cultures? Paul has to be interpreted in the light of the world in which he lived. While Jesus lived in that same world, it is not the same with him. His life (example) and teaching transcend time and circumstance. It is inconceivable that a Christian would disagree with Christ about anything. He is Lord!

Paul is not our Lord, nor was he divine, nor was he infallible even if inspired. He properly said that we should follow him as he followed Christ. We should do just that, but not more than that.

Having said that, I can say that I am uncomfortable with this whole matter of the subjugation of women to men, and submission of wives to their husbands, as in "the head of woman is man" (1 Cor. 11:3). It may have been a needed doctrine in Paul's day and perhaps for medieval times — that's what it is, medieval — but not for today's church and today's world. We should become more Christian with the passing centuries and more mature.

I do not want my wife to be submissive to me anymore than I am submissive to her. We are equals in marriage and equals in the Lord. We make decisions together, share and share alike, joys and sorrows. It impresses me as unchristian and boorish for a man to want his wife to obey him. Perhaps he should obey her. Christ has made us one, and if there is any "authority" — I dislike that word for Christians — let it be shared equally. Christ has made us one. Let's work from that truth.

What I want for the Church of Christ down the road is that there will be no social, racial, or sexual lines drawn. None whatever. Liberties and ministries will be shared equally and indiscriminately, according to gifts and talents. We must overcome the mentality that half (or more) of the church is to be subservient to the other half. All because of gender! Christ has made us one and we are all equal — and half of us are not more equal than the other half!

We must obey Christ rather than men, and if that includes Paul or the way we interpret Paul, so be it.

Chapter 19:
Effect purposeful and meaningful change, without chaos

The term "Change Without Chaos" was used at a workshop recently held at the Preston Road Church of Christ in Dallas, called "A Church That Connects." It was sponsored by Hope Network and was conducted by Lynn Anderson and Jeff Nelson. Its purpose was to instruct, inspire, and encourage Churches of Christ to be a church that "connects" by making the right kind of change. The larger-than-capacity attendance was seen as evidence of "the hunger sweeping our fellowship." It is a hunger for change. The Churches of Christ are dying for change, they said.

When I say in this installment that if the Church of Christ is to be saved it must become a changing church, I am not calling for change simply for the sake of change. The change must be positive and creative, displacing attitudes and methods that are no longer effective. The change must be in keeping with the mind of Christ, free of gimmickry, pride, and competitiveness. And it must be change without chaos, not unduly disruptive and threatening. It must be a balanced change that shows respect for the traditions of the past, the demands of the present, and the possibilities of the future.

Change! The old Greek philosophers saw change as basic to the nature of things. Heraclitus, one of the seven wise men of Athens, insisted that everything is in a state of flux. One cannot step into the same river twice, he insisted, for the river changes between steps. There would be no growth except for change. Only God changes not, and that is because he is perfect.

It is not a question of *if* we change, but *how* we change, for we are all changing all the time. So with churches. In a changing world it is essential that the church changes. It is folly to talk about being a first century church in a 21st century culture. We are to be a 21st century church with a first century faith, but not a 21st century church with a first century methodology, or even a first century view of society. Any institution that survives the centuries must change as the world around it changes or it will be ineffective. This is especially true of the church.

So, we borrow a helpful term from the Dallas workshop on change — "Change without Chaos," but we will add "but with Purpose and Meaning." That is what the Church of Christ must do to be saved: *Effect purposeful and meaningful change, free of undue disruption and chaos.* I say *undue* disruption because change cannot help but be somewhat disruptive for some people. But change need not be chaotic. We may have to rock the boat but we can avoid capsizing.

For change to be purposive it must consider the mission of the church as "the pillar and ground of the truth" in a lost and troubled world. To do this we must change the way we think about a lot of things, such as our attitude toward other religions and other churches.

Purposive change may also demand that we see ourselves in a different light, not as a people with exclusive truth but as a community of believers in a search of truth with all other communities of believers.

For change to be meaningful it must be more than cosmetic. It must actually turn us in new directions — away from the backwaters of our sectarian past. We must do more than to elect more elders and change the order of worship. We must view leadership in a different light, with elders serving not as a corporate board but as leaders among equals. We must become a church in communication with itself, with an equitable and democratic decision-making process. We must re-examine such mentalities as "the authority of the elders" and "decisions handed down by the elders." How about decisions "passed across" in a way that involves many in the congregation?

Purposive and meaningful change may call for substantial alteration in the way we view and conduct worship. We must see worship, not as an assembly to carry out certain "acts of worship," as if to conform to some check-list, but as a fellowship in the Spirit of all God's children, sharing the presence of God. We must move from seeing God as the prompter, the minister as the performer, and the congregation as the audience to seeing the minister as the prompter, the congregation as the performer, and God as the audience. Worship is to serve and praise God, not to please and satisfy ourselves. We must outgrow the mindset "to please as many in the congregation as possible" by thinking in terms of adoring and glorifying God.

The prayers of the church is a vital part of this. Rather than the wooden, predictable, repetitive prayers by the same limited number of men, Sunday after Sunday, let there be some joy, excitement, and spontaneity. And when God's family gathers to pray may only the males address the Father?

Reading of the Scriptures must also be taken more seriously, planned and prepared. It would be helpful to follow the calendar of readings used by other churches, planned so as to give a balanced diet of much of Scripture, year after year. It is one more way to share with other Christians, with all of us sharing and thinking about the same portion of the Bible, week after week. And let the women do much of the reading.

The assembly of saints is also for the building up of the church. A principle that transcends time and circumstance is: "Let all things be done for edification" (1 Cor. 14:26). Rather than thinking, "Will anyone be upset if we make this change?," let it be, "Will this edify, strengthen, and build up the church?" And this is the answer to those who resist change, those who are upset and say "That is not the way we've always done it." But it is edifying, we must learn to say.

This means we will experiment in worship, trying new things, especially ideas and methods found effective in other churches. Others have led the way in making some vital changes, and they are growing as a result. We must either lead or follow — or get out of the way, as Iacocca put it on TV.

To do all this without chaos we must lay proper ground work for change. We must not surprise people with changes, especially in worship, leading them to respond with, "What next!" We must "talk out" new ideas and methods, involving the entire congregation, before they are tried. The most effective way to do this is in small groups. When a church meets in homes once a month, which is a change many churches have recently effected, it is the ideal place to create the climate for other changes.

If a woman is to take part in a Sunday morning service for the first time ever, plans must be made well in advance. And it must not be done at all until the right climate is created and there is general agreement. This can never be realized until the leadership takes the initiative and works for change. Those with objections are to be treated with forbearance. It is to be pointed out to them that they do not have to have their way, and that it becomes a

Christian to be yielding. When such ones cannot adjust to changes that are deemed necessary for the good of the church as a whole, the congregation will have to allow such ones to go elsewhere, always of course with a love that *is* slow to let loose.

I was interested in some of the suggestions for change in the Dallas workshop, which those attending found very encouraging. The main emphasis was on "Music that makes sense," noting that for this generation music is the "coin of the realm." The workshop presented a variety of musical renditions — solo, choral, antiphonal (groups singing back and forth to each other), and congregational — with a wide variety of songs, but all acappella, with no suggestion that instruments be used in the changing Churches of Christ. Among the handouts at the workshop were dozens of new songs, some written by our own people, songs of joy and praise.

The workshop laid out a number of principles of change for the people to take back to their congregations, such as a church must first see the need for change, and change does not come without resistance. It also suggested that change will generate less heat if options are kept open. Change will not come immediately, and when it is effected it will not last unless it is carefully nurtured.

Finally, the workshop suggested how we can "think" change by realizing that there is no way for the future to be like the past. Nor will the future be what we expect it to be. It also noted that change is more likely when an atmosphere of trust is created.

For Church of Christ folk to hold a workshop on change is itself a testimonial to our capacity for change. And the workshop had to turn folk away who wanted to attend!

Don't sell our people short. The Church of Christ will be saved, after all, by effecting purposive and meaningful change, without chaos. Hopefully sooner, but, if not sooner then later.

Chapter 20:
Follow the example of churches saving themselves

In this last installment on what the Church of Christ must do to be saved I want to tell you about some congregations that are saving themselves. Their example could lead to the salvation of other congregations if they will have the courage to go and do likewise, each according to its gifts and calling.

Dallas

It is noteworthy that some of these churches are in Dallas, long considered a bastion of Church of Christ orthodoxy where any significant change would be unlikely. It was hardly predictable, for example, that the Preston Road Church of Christ, the sponsor of the once hard-line Preston Road School of Preaching, would open its facilities for a workshop on change, as it recently did, as recounted in our last installment. Or that the Skillman Ave. Church of Christ, always to the right of center, would in 1992 sponsor Restoration Forum X that hosted Christian Church leaders across the land, treating them as equals in the Lord.

And it is in Dallas, not in California (the farther west the more liberal!), that a Church of Christ has "An Ecumenical Fellowship" on its sign out front. The Central Church of Christ in Irving, not far from where the Cowboys play, is almost alone among our churches in having speakers from other denominations in its pulpit. It cooperates with other churches in numerous works of mercy.

Then there is the Richardson East Church of Christ that shares in special services with other churches. In one instance a number of their members went across town to worship with a small black Baptist church. This congregation has attracted city-wide attention, being written up in the press, for its outreach to the disenfranchised, including AIDS patients.

If I named but one church that exemplifies the changes I've pled for in this series, it might be the Lake Highlands Church of Christ in Dallas, particularly in terms of its Sunday worship service. It has made impressive strides toward the kind of Body life that the Scriptures call for, such as creating an environment where people are free to share.

They have a sharing time of some 10-15 minutes where people move about the congregation praying, confessing, and praising God together. One can see small huddles of people, circled arm in arm, all across the auditorium that seats about 600, which, by the way, they are filling. The minister explains to the visitors that this is not a time for small talk or Cowboy talk, but a time for spiritual fellowship.

A "praise team" made up of two men and two women lead the singing while the congregation stands. An overhead is used rather than hymnals. There is a choir and solos by both men and women. Testimonials by both men and women are often deeply moving. One sister told how she had a child out of wedlock when a teenager, how the Lord had rescued her, and how she could now serve meaningfully in a church that accepted and loved her. She touched the hearts of all present when she went on to tell how she had contacted her illegitimate child, who was raised in a Christian home, and received assurance from her that she had done the right thing in allowing her to be adopted. Another woman confessed her unfaithfulness to her husband, thanking God for forgiving her.

Prompted by the sad news that one of his children was getting a divorce, a longtime prominent Church of Christ preacher, one of 18 former ministers in that church who are burned out and now doing other things, got up and confessed that he had been an absentee-father and had failed his family. It was one more emotional moment for a congregation that is learning to be a confessing church, one that is learning to be compassionate. Our churches must cultivate this kind of Body life if we are to be saved.

Lake Highlands is able to move in these new directions because it has leaders who are shepherd-like and have learned to pray together. The elders gather an hour beforehand to pray for the service they will be leading. The church takes time with its rather long prayer list, with an elder leading the prayers. The church sees its elders, not as business men who are running the church or like a corporate board that hands down decisions, but as *spiritual* leaders. The minister, who teaches more than preaches, goes through the Bible, a book at a time, relating what it says to present-day needs. Aware of the great diversity in his congregation, he avoids controversial "issues," allowing the Bible itself to speak to the people.

Their position on instrumental music is that acappella singing, which they do very well, is their tradition, one to be prized, but not a biblical injunction, and they do not make it an issue. In fact they use instruments in special praise services, as well as instrumental recordings with solos.

They are breaking through the male-domination that afflicts virtually all our churches. Not only do women take part in the assembly, but some of them teach mixed adult classes. One woman, who conducts seminars for other churches, is so gifted that the elders consider themselves blessed to sit in her class.

Lake Highlands is an outreach church, with many involved in Navigators and an "Overcomers" support groups. Due to a large contingency of Cambodians in Dallas, it supports a separate church for these people. They have a "children's church" during their main assembly. They encourage their people to come up with their own ministries with the church helping out. One sister, a former airline attendant, came up with the idea of persuading American Airlines to send one of their out-of-service planes to Croatia full of food. It was done, with the church filling the plane with food! They joined two neighboring churches, Episcopalian and Disciples, in a Thanksgiving service.

A child in the church thought it would be a good idea to give gloves to homeless children in Dallas. They soon had 700 pairs to distribute! Much of the church's solidarity comes through their more intimate home gatherings, cell groups, which they have two Sunday evenings a month. They are trying to get away from their building more in their ministry and outreach.

While they do all this, they do not want their congregation to be "a neat church" where Church of Christ folk can go who are bored with where they are. They are not interested in entertaining the dissatisfied. They want to be the church, serving, witnessing, meeting people's needs, including those beyond their four walls.

El Paso and Brookline

What shall I say of other churches across the land? A few churches stand almost alone in the changes they have made. The Downtown Church of Christ in El Paso, for example, is the only Church of Christ that I know of that has adopted instrumental music in its assembly that is still a Church of Christ. Women also minister from the pulpit. It is half Anglo, half Hispanic, and they minister to the poor on both sides of the Rio Grande. It has the distinction of being a non-instrument Church of Christ, with an ACU-educated minister, that has an instrument!

Then there is the Brookline Church of Christ in Massachusetts, near Harvard and M.I.T., that published a statement a few years back that it had resolved, after much study and prayer, that it would allow gifts to determine ministry, not sex. Women do all that the men do, including the pulpit ministry and serving as elders, except that the church has a steering committee instead of elders, two of which are women. Women graduate students have served as ministers.

The leaders are uneasy when there are visitors from the South and a woman is in the pulpit, for they do not want to shock people. But sometimes the visitors surprise them, even those presumed to be hardliners. One such visitor, after hearing a woman preach, commented on how uplifting the service was. The leaders there say that we all lose much in not allowing women to lead prayers, for they often pray with more urgency and about things that do not concern men. Some say that we do not really know what worship is until women have a part.

The church follows the church year in its readings and celebration of such holy days as Christmas and Easter, and they have union services with other churches. While they are acappella in their congregational singing, they use instruments on special occasions. Baptism by immersion is taught and practiced, but they do not have a membership directory as such and immersion is not required for acceptance.

Names are added to their list of "Members and Friends" as people become regular in attendance. Some decide to be immersed long after being a part of the congregation, others may never. This is closely kin to "open membership," openly rare among Churches of Christ but *de facto* not all that uncommon.

We are all indebted to Brookline, long a haven for our graduate students, including Ouida and me when I was at Harvard, for coming to grips with our tradition rather than leaving it, and it is easier to leave, as many do, than to deal with it. They have dealt with it and have remained a Church of Christ, in unity with all the rest of us in things that really matter. They say in their bulletin that they are part of the Restoration Movement.

Tulsa

Then there is the minister who recently applied for a job at the Southern Hills Church of Christ in Tulsa and brought a "Position Paper" along with him, which he passed out to the congregation. In it he stated that he favored acappella singing, but he would not be preaching against instrumental music if hired, that "It is not a biblical subject and certainly not a matter of fellowship." There were also disclaimers to a legalistic position on baptism, the ministry of women, and the Holy Spirit. He also said that he was not "a Church of Christ preacher" and stated that he was open to fellowship with other churches. He said he is proud of his Restoration roots and wants to stay with Churches of Christ, but not controlled by them. He wants to help lead our people out of "the paralysis of sectarianism." I tell you all this to tell you the big news. He was hired!

Lubbock

I've saved the best for the last, or at least the most unusual. Hold on to your seat for this one. The Quaker Avenue Church of Christ in Lubbock, a non-Sunday School congregation, sent the following letter to the Broadway Church of Christ, the largest and most influential Sunday School church in the same city:

We, the elders of the Quaker Avenue Church of Christ, have for some time been grieved over the separations within the Body of Christ. While there have been steps taken in recent years to move away from the animosities of the past, there are still settled divisions among us. We, for instance, from those churches which do not favor or employ Sunday Schools, have not had much fellowship with those who do. We have frequently been regarded as "anti" brethren, and sometimes scorned as being backward and legalistic for a position we take on the basis of genuine concern for scripture. It is true that we differ in this respect from many other brethren, but we do not feel that such difference should keep us from brotherly relations in the numerous areas where we hold mutual ground.

They went on in the letter to refer to the debates of the past and all the ugly divisions. They did not want to judge on who was responsible for the divisions, but that they felt responsible "to bring about greater unity in our day." They stated that while they had not caused the divisions they had helped to maintain them. "We repent of that and seek the forgiveness of God and all our brethren," they went on to say. While they regretted all the grief that some of their people had caused in the past, they were thankful for their heritage and all the good things handed down to them.

They said that while they sought closer association "with brethren who differ with us on the Sunday School, we do not renounce our fathers in the faith." They went on to make a statement that should be heralded among all our churches, one that beautifully reflects what the Stone-Campbell movement was all about:

From this time forth we want to be known as a people who love all the brethren. We believe that honest difference need not divide us, that we can enjoy sweet fellowship in all that we mutually hold dear while allowing for some diversity in interpretation and practice. Our plea for reconciliation is not by any means a repudiation of our position on Sunday Schools, but a recognition that such issues are less important than the blood of Jesus that made us one.

They went on to ask for "the right hand of fellowship" from the Broadway church, and added, "May our rich heritage in the Restoration Movement, which began as an attempt to unite all Christians, be rekindled today in new demonstration of the noble principles of our past. More importantly, let us fulfill the prayer of our Lord, who wanted us all to be one in order that the world might believe."

I understand that the Broadway elders were delightfully surprised to receive such a letter and responded in kind (see Appendix III). The two churches will be looking for things they can do together, but what is important is that they have accepted each other as equals in the Lord in spite of differences, which happens to be the only way to accept each other in the Lord!

I consider this one of the most significant documents of our Movement's recent history. I hope either the Quaker Ave. church or the Broadway church will put it in pamphlet form and distribute it far and wide (see Appendix IV). It will serve to heal the wounds of our fragmented people. Let each faction among us have the spirit of Quaker Ave. Each division among us could and should write the same letter, and in place of "Sunday School" insert the "issue" that is the cause of rupture, whether instrumental music, Herald of Truth, premillennialism, plurality of cups, etc.

Conclusion

These are but a few of the changing churches among us. What does all this mean? It means that we can all change for the better if we have the will. It also means that the Churches of Christ are a beautiful people with lots of creative diversity. It means that we should recognize our diversity and accept the liberating truth that oneness does not mean sameness.

We can have churches that have Sunday School and those that do not; those that support Herald of Truth and those that do not; those that have instrumental music and those that do not; those that use plurality of cups and those that do not; churches that are premillennial and those that are not, etc., etc., and yet be united in the essentials of the faith, and doing at least some things together. And no one has to compromise any truth or violate his or her conscience!

If we are to be saved as a people and recapture our heritage as a unity movement, we have no choice but to get with it.

Endnotes

1. This article is known in Latin as *Dignitatis humanae*. At the time of this publication it was available in English on the web site of the Holy See at: http://www.vatican.va/archive/hist_councils/ii_vatican_council/documents/vat-ii_decl_19651207_dignitatis-humanae_en.html

2. At the time of this publication, the *Campbell-Rice Debate* was available for viewing at the following URL: http://www.archive.org/stream/campbellricedeba00campiala#page/n3/mode/2up

3. D. A. Carson, "Reflections on the Book *I Just Want to be a Christian*, by Dr. Rubel Shelly." Written at the request of The Foundation for Advanced Biblical Studies (FABS) International, Inc., 1988. At the time of this publication the article is located online at: http://www.mun.ca/rels/restmov/texts/rmeyes/carson.html

4. At the time of this publication this document was available at the following URL:

http://www.mun.ca/rels/restmov/texts/moser/
AWPTG.HTM

Appendix I

AN ADDRESS TO THE CHURCHES OF CHRIST.

by Barton W. Stone

I am now near three score years of age — near 36 of which I have labored in word and doctrine. I labored seven years with the Presbyterians, and should have continued with them, if they had permitted me to read and understand the scriptures for myself, and to preach them according to my understanding of them. But this I was not permitted to do. Honesty I preferred to hypocrisy, liberty to slavery, poverty to wealth, a good conscience to ease and popularity, and the glory of God, and the honor of his truth, to every other consideration: therefore, with a few free spirits, I resigned all my friends, my ease, my good name, my living, to Jesus and his truth; determined to follow him wherever his word should direct me. To be bound by a human authoritative creed, confessed to be fallible, I could not, I would not. — Determined to be free myself, I durst not attempt to impose such a creed on others.

I thought, if Presbyterians had a divine warrant to exclude me and my brethren from the ministry, because we could not conscientiously receive and preach their peculiar doctrines, then must they have a divine warrant to exclude every other sect that does not receive and preach their doctrines. If they have not this right to exclude other sects, they had none to exclude us. — All sects claim this right; and were they to act up to it, they would be mutually excluded, by one another. Can this be of God? As much so, as the claims of the Pope to infallibility. I confess I see no difference, unless it be this, that the Pope boldly claims to be infallible; but the sects deny infallibility in word, but act upon the principles of infallibility; for they exclude from the kingdom (such they call their sectarian establishments) all who cannot receive and proclaim the doctrines of their creed. Would they dare do this, did they really think that their creed was not infallible?

There are two kinds of human authoritative creeds — one is drawn up in articles, and written or printed in a book — the other is a set of doctrines or opinions received, but not committed to writing, or printed in a book. Each of these kinds of creeds is used for the same purpose, which is to exclude from fellowship the man, who dares to dissent from them. Of the two, we certainly give the preference to creeds written and published; because we can then read them, and form a more correct judgment of the doctrines contained in them.

There are some amongst us very clamorous against written or printed creeds, who yet have a creed of their own, of which they are as tenacious, as any other sectarian is of his written creed; and they are equally intolerant against those who dissent from their doctrines or opinions. From several sources we have received accounts of some (I am sorry to say teachers too) who have received it as an article of their unwritten creed that none should be baptized, but such as are saved, and have their sins forgiven, and who have in themselves the evidence of that forgiveness and salvation. These teachers, therefore, oppose zealously those who act up to the old commission, "preach the gospel to every creature. He that believeth and is baptized shall *be saved* — and repent and be baptized for the remission of sins, etc." Do they preach that a man must be saved from his sins, and must have his sins remitted before baptism? This is their creed; and the plain scripture to the contrary must be frittered away, in order that their creed may stand securely.

I have no doubt that many brethren, who differ on this subject, do not understand it. Disputations, founded on ignorance, are generally very warm, and always endless. Many advocates for the doctrine of being baptized for the remission of sins have, by their ignorance of the doctrine, done infinite injury to the cause, and have given just reason to others to be alarmed, and to oppose their real error. And these opposers have done equal injury to the cause, and have by their unguarded, not to say, unchristian zeal, given just cause to others to be offended. My dear contending brethren, will you candidly attend to an old servant and brother, while he pleads for reconciliation?

Does the advocate for remission of sins by baptism, plead that by baptism the heart of a sinner is changed — that he is saved from the love and reign of sin? If he does, he is entirely ignorant of the doctrine for this change must take place before he is a fit subject for baptism. He must believe and repent or reform, before he should be baptized. And what is reformation but a change of heart? Can a man be said to be reformed from sin, and yet love sin? No. He cannot. By faith in Jesus, who lived, died and rose again, the sinner is reconciled to God, and consequently, hates sin, and is determined to reform and turn from all iniquity, and obey God in all things. Yet he is not saved from the condemnation of sin, his sins are not yet remitted or forgiven. He is therefore commanded by the authority of Jesus to be baptized for the remission of sins, for salvation. He submits to be baptized, and now the pardoning act of God is passed, he is forgiven, wrath and guilt are removed.

A poor criminal is chained in jail, condemned to be hung. The Governor offers to save him from this penalty of death, or to remit or forgive his sin, which is the same thing as to save him from being hung, provided he will reform and be immersed. The terms are proposed — the poor criminal seeing the mercy, goodness and favor of the governor, is brought to contrition and melted to tears. He is heartily determined on reformation — O, says he, I am determined to sin no more. I do and will reform. Is he now forgiven? No: he has complied with but one term — he must be immersed in water. He does not cavil, but immediately is immersed — now he is pardoned. Now says he, I am saved from the gallows — now my sin is remitted. I know I am forgiven, if the word of the governor be true. So says the poor repentant sinner, who in the name of Jesus is immersed for the remission of sins. Baptism is a confirmation and seal of his pardon.

What we understand by reformation then is a change of heart: this by some is called regeneration. With such I have no dispute while we believe the same thing. Regeneration we believe is a change of our state, and not of our heart. — It is to be inducted into the kingdom of God — into the full privileges of the new dispensation.

But is nothing more necessary besides faith, reformation and immersion? Yes; "And you shall receive the gift of the Holy Spirit." This is the crowning blessing of all blessings. This Spirit we are said to *receive through faith.* Gal. 3, 14. *"This Spirit is also given to them that obey him."* Acts, 5, 32. — It is given *to them that ask him.* God's plan appears to be this, that whoever believes, reforms, is baptized, or obeys the gospel shall be saved, shall receive remission of sins, and the gift of the Holy Spirit.

But, says the opposer of the doctrine, "Is baptism regeneration?" I answer; no, not in your understanding of the word, as meaning a change of heart; this change we think is reformation, which must precede baptism.

But, you may still say, can God forgive none but the immersed? We are assured he will forgive the immersed penitent, because his word has assured us he will. We cannot be so sure that he will forgive the unimmersed penitent. Could a person be brought by doctrine to believe that faith and repentance were only necessary to remission, and that baptism was entirely unnecessary to this effect, he might receive this word with gladness, and this he might take for evidence of remission; but we should ask the important question, what saith the scripture? We have no doubt that multitudes have been changed, are pious, and will ultimately be saved with an everlasting salvation who have not been immersed. We are far from saying, that God has so bound himself by his plan, that he cannot pardon an humble penitent without immersion! Far from us be this sentiment.

But say some; Campbellism we will oppose. In this we wish you success. But beware lest you are either beating the air, not understanding what it is; or lest you oppose the truth of God, because bro. Campbell has advocated it. There is danger, and therefore, you ought to be cautious. But says another, I am determined to oppose Stone's Arianism, and Socinianism, with all my might — Amen! But be sure, you fight not an image made by yourself or by others, and call it Stone's doctrine; and beware lest in your opposition you lift your arm against the truth of God and do a great injury to yourself. Campbell and Stone are but fallible men, and therefore should not be followed farther than they follow Christ. Our opinions we wish no man to receive as truth, nor do we desire to impose them on any as tests of christian fellowship. This is the principle on which we as christians commenced our course many years ago, and I cannot but view those as departed from this principle, who will not bear with their brethren, because they believe in baptism for the remission of sins, and because they meet every Lord's day to worship the Lord in praying, singing, exhorting, and breaking bread. O brethren, these are subjects concerning which many of us differ, but for this difference we ought not separate from communion, and christian fellowship. All believe that immersion is baptism — why should they who submit to the one baptism contend and separate because they do not exactly view every design of it alike?

We have opposition and war from every sect. They appear to be combined against us. Shall we fight one another? — We, who profess to stand upon the Bible alone, and contend that opinions of truth should not be made terms of fellowship — shall we be intolerant towards each other because we may differ in our opinions? Forbid it, Heaven! If you think your brother in error, labor in the spirit of love and meekness to convince him; but imposing zeal against him will only harden him against any good impression you would make. It will probably stir up strife, and ultimately destroy love, the bond of union. Preach the word, was an apostolic command to a young preacher. It would be well for us all to attend to it diligently. In doing this we shall both save ourselves and others: this cannot be done by preaching our opinions. Let the unity of christians be our polar star. To this let our eyes be continually turned, and to this let our united efforts be directed — that the world may believe, and be saved. A little longer forbearance with each others weakness, and truth will triumph. But let that man, who opposes christian union, remember, that he opposes the prayer of Jesus, and the salvation of the world. How will he meet his Judge?

B. W. Stone, Editor.

Appendix II

QUAKER AVE. CHURCH OF CHRIST

1701 QUAKER   PHONE 792-0652

LUBBOCK, TEXAS 79416

"Exalting Christ in Worship and Service"

April 12, 1992

The Elders
Broadway Church of Christ
Lubbock, Texas

Greetings in the name of our common Lord:

We, the elders of the Quaker Avenue Church of Christ, have for some time been grieved over the separations within the Body of Christ. While there have been steps taken in recent years to move away from the animosities of the past, there are still settled divisions among us. We, for instance, of those churches which do not favor or employ Sunday Schools, have not had much fellowship with those who do. We have frequently been regarded as "anti" brethren, and sometimes scorned as being backward and legalistic for a position we take on the basis of genuine concern for the scripture. It is true that we differ in this respect from many other brethren, but we no longer feel that such difference should keep us from brotherly relations in the numerous areas where we hold mutual ground.

We are aware of the debates and strife of the past that often led to our divisions. Most of us were not here then and we do not feel we can appropriately judge who was responsible for the division. But we are convinced that we the living are responsible for doing whatever is possible to bring about greater unity in our day. We want you to know that we all are genuinely sorry for whatever led to division, knowing what a hindrance it has been to the cause of Christ. While we did not ourselves contribute to the original division, some of us have, in our own lifetime, been guilty of attitudes that have maintained it. We repent of that and seek the forgiveness of God and all our brethren. As we look back and recall the rancor and bitterness that has often existed, we are grieved and to such extent as we and our brethren have been responsible, we seek forgiveness.

At the same time, we are thankful for many good things in our heritage, and the good men and women who engendered and cultivated our faith. They were not perfect, but they gave us much. In seeking better relations with brethren who differ with us on the Sunday School, we do not renounce our fathers in the faith. We simply wish to acknowledge and embrace the whole family of God, and thereby renounce sectarianism and the party spirit.

From this time forth, we want to be known as *a* people who love the brethren. We believe that honest difference need not divide us, that we can enjoy sweet fellowship in all that we mutually hold dear while allowing for some diversity in interpretation and practice. Our plea for reconciliation is not by any means a repudiation of our position on Sunday Schools, but a recognition that such issues are less important than the blood of Jesus that made us one. We are willing to discuss our understanding in these matters with anyone, but we do not intend to impose our views upon you or others. Nor do we feel it is necessary to wait until we reach perfect agreement to enjoy fellowship in Christ. The Apostle Paul tells us to "accept one another, just as Christ accepts [us], in order to bring praise to God" (Rom. 15:7). It is likely that when we walk together as brethren, we can discuss our differences in an atmosphere that is more conducive to understanding and agreement. Our divisions will never be healed if we continue to treat each other as enemies instead of as brethren in the same family.

What we are asking from you is the right hand of fellowship in the great work of the kingdom. While you may still regard us as a bit "quaint" in some of our views, let us at least be regarded as brethren. Especially in this centennial year of Churches of Christ in Lubbock, let us proclaim together the grace that makes us one in Jesus. And let us together extend the same spirit of fellowship to all of our other brethren, all who in faith have been born of water and the spirit, and who earnestly seek to follow Jesus. May our rich heritage in the Restoration Movement, which began as an attempt to unite all Christians, be rekindled today in new demonstration of the noble principles of our past. More importantly, let us fulfill the prayer of our Lord, who wanted us all to be one in order that the world might believe (John. 17:21).

We have considered the prayer of Paul and we want to experience what he desired: "May the God who gives endurance and encouragement give you a spirit of unity among yourselves as you follow Christ Jesus, so that with one heart and mouth you may glorify the God and Father of our Lord Jesus Christ" (Rom. 15:5-6). We pledge you our hearts and hands, as brothers in Christ Jesus.

The Elders
Quaker Avenue Church of Christ
1701 Quaker Avenue
Lubbock, Texas 79416

Appendix III

Broadway Church of Christ

1924 Broadway • Lubbock, Texas 79401 • (A.C. 806) 763-0464

To the Elders
Quaker Avenue Church of Christ
1701 Quaker Avenue
Lubbock, Texas 79416

May 1, 1992

Dear Brothers:

We, too, want to be unified with all of those who are brethren so "that the world might believe" (John 17:21) Jesus was sent from our Father God. We, too, want to experience the desire of Paul in proclaiming "the God who gives endurance and encouragement give you a spirit of unity among yourselves as you follow Jesus Christ, so that with one heart and mouth you may glorify the God and Father of our Lord Jesus Christ" (Romans 15:56). We were all thrilled and elated to receive your recent letter asking for fellowship together in the work of the Kingdom.

We unanimously and enthusiastically want fellowship with all of the brothers and sisters who are part of the Quaker Avenue church family, as well as all who by faith through grace have been born of water and the spirit and who are seeking to be disciples of Jesus Christ our Lord. It is officially in our minutes that we are in fellowship with you.

We think it would be good to communicate this renewal to all who are part of our church family here at Broadway. We plan to let our people know as soon as possible.

We understand from several who attended the recent elders/ministers banquet at Sunset that Thomas Langford made a very touching and moving plea for brotherly love and unity among all who were present. We think that was a marvelous action and we commend and admire the spirit in which it was done.

We will be looking forward to visiting with you about some kind of joint congregational activity or sharing pulpit time or something creative that will demonstrate in action what we have said in our hearts and on paper. Please know of our love and respect for you as leaders among God's people. We are thankful for your tender and expressive hearts and give glory to God for His work in you. We ask for your continual prayers and encouragement as well and may God continue to be praised through our loving one another.

For the Broadway Shepherds,

Noel Ellis
Rod Blackwood
Joe Burks
Shepherd's Administrative Team

Appendix IV

From: David Langford
<dlangford@quakeravenue.com>
To: blewis@limestone.edu
Priority: Normal
Subject: Letter
Date: Tue 03/08/10 2:02 PM

Brother Lewis,

I am happy to send you the letter Leroy referred to. In addition to that I will also send you the gracious letter which the Broadway church sent in response. As a result of this correspondence our congregation at Quaker Avenue and the Broadway church held three joint services over the next few years that were wonderful events. The letters were exchanged in 1991 and that correspondence has led to a warm and cooperative relationship that continues to this day. One of the fruits of that relationship was our joint sponsorship, along with the Vandelia Church of Christ, First Christian Church (Disciples of Christ) and

Raintree Christian Church (Independent Christian), of the 2002 Restoration Forum. I have also enclosed a copy of the "Unity Pledge" which was signed by several hundred at that event.

This is more than you asked for, but as the Lord once told us, we often get responses that are pressed down, shaken together and running over." :)

Blessings

David

(See Unity Pledge next page)

A Unity Covenant

Pledging ourselves to be part of the answer
to our Lord's prayer for unity among
believers in Christ

*May they be brought to complete
unity to let the world know that you
sent me and have loved them even as you
have loved me.*
John 17:23

**As disciples of Jesus, we covenant together,
by God's grace,**

To share our Lord's passion and urgency for
unity among believers as demonstrated in his
prayer before going to the cross (John 17:20-26)

To recognize the importance of unity among ourselves to be able to successfully communicate the gospel to the world (John 13:34, 35)

To turn away from any kind of divisive or factious spirit which is not characteristic of the spirit of Christ (Galatians 5:20)

To acknowledge that while we may differ in our approach and understanding of what Christian unity requires, such differences should not prevent us from making every effort to do what leads to greater peace and understanding among us (Romans 14:19)

"In faith unity,
in opinion liberty,
in all things love"

Restoration

Forum XX

October 20-22,
2002
Lubbock, Texas

Other Kindle books from SCM *e*-Prints:

Declaration and Address & The Last Will and Testament, by Thomas Campbell and Barton W. Stone
   ASIN: B0043M6JP6

A Pilgrimage of Joy, by W. Carl Ketcherside
   ASIN: B003XNU0PQ

The Death of the Custodian, by W. Carl Ketcherside
   ASIN: B003YJEWLW

The Twisted Scriptures, by W. Carl Ketcherside
   ASIN: B002LLO912

See complete list at: www.Stone-Campbell.org

Made in the USA
San Bernardino, CA
29 July 2014